Devon Warriner ---------- Get

GET OVER IT

By
Devon Warriner

To Angela — Enjoy! Devon

MARSHALL MICHIGAN
WWW.800PUBLISHING.COM

Devon Warriner   ----------   Get Over it

Get Over it
Copyright © 2009 by Devon Warriner
\
Cover design by   2 Moon Press
                    307 West Michigan Ave
                    Marshall MI 49068

Author photo by   Digital Designs

The opinions expressed in this manuscript are solely the opinions of the author and do not represent the opinions or thoughts of the publisher. The author represents and warrants that s/he either owns or has the legal right to publish all material in this book.

ISBN-13: 978-0-9826020-7-2
ISBN-10: 0-9826020-7-3

First published in 2010

10 9 8 7 6 5 4 3 2 1

Published by   2 MOON PRESS
                    307 1/2 W. Michigan Ave, Marshall MI 49068
                    www.800publishing.com

All Rights Reserved. This book may not be reproduced, transmitted, or stored in whole or in part by any means, including graphic, electronic, or mechanical without the express written consent of the publisher except in the case of brief quotations embodied in critical articles and reviews.

PRINTED IN THE UNITED STATES OF AMERICA

Special Thanks

To my favorite authors – I've cried and rejoiced with your characters. I've lived my life alongside theirs. I've experienced things with them I haven't experienced on my own. Thanks for making it possible for me to write what I do and giving me the experiences I need.

To some of my best friends – You better know who you are, but thanks to Emily Campau, Kaitlin Frazier, Lauren Varvatos, and Alex Veale. Whether you gave me input or ideas, you helped in some way with this story and the telling of it. Thanks for being great friends and supporting my dreams.

To my family – Mom and Dad, Grandma, Aunt Shirley, and everyone else. Mom and Dad: I love you! You've been great parents for all of my life, and I'm glad you're my parents. Thanks for helping me reach one of my goals. Grandma: thanks for going through this story with me and giving me more ideas, along with editing a little. Everyone who reads my book can know the characters a little better because of your help. Thanks for being my sponsor for Confirmation last year, and thanks for being one of my inspirations. I'm glad you're my grandmother. Love you! Aunt Shirley: you're the reason we go to Mackinac Island every summer. Without you, I wouldn't have been able to write this story. Thanks for making that possible. I love you, too. Andrew: I'm glad you're excited my book is coming out. I love when you bring it up to me. Love you! Everyone else (grandparents, aunts, uncles, cousins, and distant relatives): thanks for the support and the amazement that I wrote a book. I love you all.

To 2 Moon Press – Thanks for all the work on my manuscript and the cover. Publishing my book was a good experience, thanks to you.

Devon Warriner

March 2010

Devon Warriner   ----------   Get Over it

Devon Warriner ---------- Get Over it

Maddi Andrews
English 11
Hour 6
5/30/08

Friends

    Bridget was my best friend. She was the greatest artist I knew, and a good storywriter too. She was always a little distracted, a little slow to catch on, but she was so good with any details. Ask her to describe someone and you would have gotten the fullest description ever. She was so cool that way.

    Every summer, Bridget and her family would spend a week with my family on Mackinac Island. We would bike around, eat out for lunch, make dinner at the cottage, shop, and eat fudge. It is always so much fun to go on vacation with a close person that is not related to you. However, she will not be able to come this year. No, it is not her parents' fault, or her own. Unfortunately this year it is just how it is. This summer was going to be the best one ever for me and Bridget. A couple years ago, we convinced our parents to let us ride horses. We talked so much about how we were going to do more this time. We were going to cook dinner one night (because it was going to be fun), ride horses by ourselves (well, we would have a guide, but no parents), bike around the island by ourselves, and have our own adventures. All that changed a few months ago. I used to look forward to this trip, but now I am dreading it.

    Bridget's thirteen-year-old brother called me one night in February, telling me to come to the hospital. He said that he had known I would want to be there with Bridget. He explained that she had been in a car accident and was not likely to survive. I arrived there shortly after she had, so I had almost two hours with her before she passed, but that was not enough time to say a proper goodbye, and my heart already ached to have her back.

    After I got home from the hospital, my mom came into my room to talk to me. She sat down on my bed and asked me if I wanted to know exactly what happened to Bridget. I remember sitting there, my heart racing, feeling so scared. Did I really want to know "exactly" what happened? Did I really want to live her death? I took a deep breath and told her yes. My voice wobbled when I said the word. My mom looked at me, placing a hand on my knee. She took a deep breath and spoke.

    Bridget died in her car with her boyfriend, Adam, while he was driving. They were such a cute couple and always seemed to be together doing something. That is, whenever Bridget and I were not doing anything. Bridget was in the passenger seat, and they were on their way to a movie. It had just rained earlier, and it was getting colder. Soon it would be cold enough to freeze, so the roads were a little slick. Adam was always a careful driver, especially in bad weather. Bridget and Adam were a block away from the theater, waiting at a light. It finally turned green, so Adam started moving again, driving in his careful way. When he was right in the middle of the intersection, a truck came from the other road and smashed into Bridget's side. It could not have stopped; it was simply going too fast and the driver was drunk. Bridget was rushed to the hospital, along with Adam, and her car was pushed to the side of the road. Adam had a broken wrist from hitting it on the wheel, a bruised eye from hitting his face somewhere, and was obviously sore, but Bridget was severely injured and died within two hours at the hospital.

    My mom sat there looking at me for a long time. I glanced at her and then cried again. I pictured Bridget laughing in the car, wondering what the movie would be like. Her life was over because someone wanted to drive when they were drunk. My friend would never have another summer in Mackinac because someone wanted to drive drunk.

    Part of my heart died with Bridget that night, February 22. I almost went to Mackinac alone this year. After all, how could it be the same without Bridget? But I needed someone to help me see the sights, do the things Bridget and I were going to do, and help me deal with her being gone. So I am bringing Holly, another great friend, but it will not be the same. We will not have the same freedom, because she has only been to Mackinac Island once, during our fourth grade trip there, and does not know the lay of the land. I am going to miss Bridget. My life will never be the same. Every day will be different.

    Bridget's funeral was a few days after the accident. I could not stand to be in the room. I have been to several funerals, so I thought I could handle this one, but it was different. Most of the funerals I have been to, I did not really know the person or I was too young to understand. The only other person I was close to whose funeral I went to was my Grandma Katie's. I was only three then, so I did not understand what we were doing. As soon as I walked up to Bridget's casket, I started crying. Her big cappuccino-colored eyes were closed, and her brown hair was neatly arranged. She was ghostly pale. I had to leave because I was going to cry. Actually, I was going to sob and I felt like screaming. So I said my final words to her. Then I leaned over the edge to kiss her head like a parent might do to a child to say goodnight, but I was saying goodbye. Not even for just a short while, but goodbye for forever. I ran into the bathroom and cried the rest of the funeral. My friends, Holly and Emily, soon appeared to comfort me. Neither of them were as close to Bridget as I was, but they felt my pain too. No words were needed between the three of us. We just sat on the floor, in each other's company, feeling a comfort no words could give. Bridget meant a lot to me, nobody can understand how much. No one will ever understand how deep our friendship was, how deeply we were connected. On February 22, Bridget died, and so did part of me. I hope and pray that this does not happen to anyone else. No one should have to go through this suffering when they are only seventeen years old.

  This story must seem really tragic to anyone reading this paper. Well, that is true. But I learned something. True friends mean the most to you and you will never forget them. If they disappeared tomorrow, you would remember them forever, and you would probably mope around a bit. That is exactly what I did, and I am still doing it, but I have tried to forget all of this when I go to school and do my homework. Doing this particular assignment does not help, but at the same time it does. It is making me cry, and remember all the good times I shared with Bridget, so I am sad, but writing my feelings will probably help me get over this moping sooner. Friends mean the world to everyone. The proof lies in this story.

Devon Warriner   ----------   Get Over it

June 10th
Family Acadia

Dear Journal,

    Holly is coming to Mackinac Island with my family and me this summer. We're already more than halfway there by driving. I bet Holly can't wait to see the island. It's been seven years since she has gone, and she was only there for a day. I guess it's nice to have someone else come on vacation with me, but I'm going to miss Bridget. Everything's changing. I don't want it to. We're even staying for more than a week. Aunt Shelly gave us Dufina Cottage, the house we stay in every summer, for the rest of the month. I think she got an extra month so she could stay longer, but couldn't do two months. Holly and I are going to look for jobs, since we have the time and it would be nice to make some money.

    And oh, yeah! It's Holly's birthday today. She turned 17 years old!

    I wonder if we'll do all the traditions on the island. Doing the puzzle and playing dominoes and such...

I bet Dad will continue his traditions of riding around the island almost daily and a few midnight rides. But I bet he'll get tired after a while.

Last year, Dad decided he wanted to swim in Lake Huron. He wanted to take an inner tube, and decided to inflate it at home, then ride to the lake with it on his back. On the way back to the cottage, he rode by a horse, who got spooked and broke part of the carriage. The carriage driver was pretty upset. When Dad got home, he told us about his adventure, and our whole family wondered if it would be the talk of the town and even show up in the newspaper. It didn't, but there *was* a story about a plastic bag spooking a horse downtown. I hope Dad won't try that again…

"Hey! Maddi, get your nose out of your journal! What kingdom are algae from? I can't remember!" Holly asked, pointing her stylus at her pink Nintendo DS Lite. Her inquiry showed in her gray-green eyes.

"Protista. But put protists because that's what that game recognizes it as." I answered, not taking my eyes off my notebook.

"Yay!" Holly cheered, "I won a million dollars! I'm smarter than a fifth-grader," she added sarcastically.

"I knew the answer to that!" my thirteen year old brother teased.

"Yeah, 'cause you learned it last year. We, on the other hand, can't remember everything we ever learned," Holly shot back.

"Hey! Look! There's the parking lot for Arnold ferry!" my mom said. We pulled into the unloading area where they tag everything as it gets pulled out of your car. My brother got out right away. "Luke! Get back here and help us unpack!" Holly and I grabbed our backpacks and then helped unload. It took a while since we always bring so much food, clothing, and stuff to do. We were almost done when the ferry came in, and they were told to wait for us and another family. We rushed onto the ship and sat in the red cushioned chairs on the first level. Luke and Dad went to the top level, where it was super windy. They were the only ones in our family who enjoyed the wind.

"Where's the Annex?" Holly asked when we were on the island. She was reading a red tag attached to our luggage.

"It's the street our cottage is on. It's behind the Grand Hotel. You have to go up a really big hill." I answered, without thinking about it. People often asked where Dufina Cottage was. It was such an automatic response. I've been answering it since I was seven years old. And I answered that question at least ten times in the same day when I was on my fourth grade trip and wanted to show my friends where I lived for a week of my summer. Well, Bridget answered some of their questions too, to give me a rest from talking, since I don't like to talk that much. She's been coming for our week since she was in the third grade.

I stopped thinking and looked up to the main street and inhaled. The smell unique to Mackinac Island filled my nose, and my eyes took in the familiar sights once again. A few "taxis" were waiting for people right in front of us, and a girl was sitting at the tiny bike rental business looking bored. Taxis on Mackinac Island were carriages pulled by horses. Most of the taxis weren't as fancy as the word "carriages" makes them sound. Many people wandered around on the sidewalk, trying to find their way to one place or another.

"Maddi, come on!" Luke was already sitting on one of the seats of the dray that was going to take our stuff up so we could bike up ourselves. Up next to the driver, staring at the horses' butts, to be exact.

"Come on where? You have to ride your bike too! Get ready! And hurry up!" I teased as he jumped down and his foot landed in horse you-know-what. One of the very common accidents people have on this island. The sound he made was a little sickening smack, but trust Luke to just jump up and stick his tongue out. We set out for our cottage on our bikes as soon as he was done cleaning his shoe. We hit the Grand Hotel hill fast. It's a really big, steep hill that causes most people to get off their bikes and walk the rest of the way up. I usually make it up without stopping once, but I stayed with Holly who was pretty slow. Luke made it up without stopping. It's his first time doing that. I can already tell he'll brag.

"Did you see that?" Luke asked, super excited when we reached Dufina. He was very sweaty, and his muddy brown hair was sticking up in every direction.

"Yes." Holly answered. I can't believe how proud he is! Of course, he lost a lot of weight since we last came. Everybody started teasing him for being overweight, so he started working out and eating healthier, because he already loved playing sports.

"Hello?" I heard two people say. I jolted out of my trance with Luke's face right in front of me. His slightly too-big nose, thin lips, wide forehead, and brown eyes were a little scary that close to my face.

"What? Oh, yeah," I said, dazed. Just then I saw a flash of something in the trees behind Luke, between Dufina and the newer house next door. I grabbed Holly, she grabbed our stuff, and we raced into the house, through the kitchen and dining room, up the stairs and dashed into the pink bedroom I assumed was ours. The walls, dresser and the two twin bed frames were painted pink, and the covers to the bed were pink, also. The comforter, though white, had pink on it, too.

"Whoa! What's with the rush?" Holly asked.

"Well, two reasons. One- I wanted to show you the house! Two- I saw something outside."

"What was that something?" she asked. I shot her a look and shrugged.

"I don't know. It was probably a bat, but I didn't want to find out!"

After we unpacked our stuff in our bedroom, I showed Holly around the rest of the upstairs. There were three other bedrooms besides ours. Right next to the pink room, there was another bedroom which had a double bed, a braided floor rug and wooden plank walls. Down the hall was the blue bedroom, which had blue walls, blue rug and cream and blue on the bedspread, and then the Master bedroom, the largest one, that had a queen bed, braided floor rugs and also had wooden plank walls. There was a small bathroom off the hallway that had a really old type of sink and clawfoot bathtub. To get to the other bathroom that had a shower, we went through the master bedroom. I showed Holly the trick to using the shower, which was hanging over another clawfoot tub.

Holly and I then went back downstairs, into the main living room, which was a really large room with a mixture of antique furniture and bigger, more comfortable furniture. It also had the out-of-tune piano that no one played. I took her out the front door of the house onto the big, wrap around front porch. The front porch was a great place to curl up and read. We came back into the house, through the living room, into the small family room that had the only TV in the house, and a large, old fireplace. The big round coffee table was in the family room, which is where we did our annual 1000 piece puzzle every summer. Past the family room was the small dining room which we often used for playing games. It had a large, heavy wooden table, with two long wooden benches. The benches had long green cushions on them that usually got annoying, since they would slip off the bench as we were sitting on them. We rounded the corner to go back into the kitchen, so we could stop on the back porch and grab some pop from the coolers that we kept there. The porch also had the dryer, which I always though was an interesting place to put it. We headed back through the formal dining room and ran upstairs to our pink room so we could start making our list of places to look for jobs.

Places to Ask for Jobs

1. The old French Outpost (now the Gate House)
2. The Gift Horse –Me
3. Yankee Rebel Tavern –Me
4. That ice cream place (Fred's?)
5. Ryba's fudge shop –Holly
6. The bike place by Arnold Ferry
7. The other fudge places (Murdick's, Joann's, etc.) –Holly

"Where are we asking first?" Holly asked staring at the list.
"Um, well, I'll show you to a fudge place, then go to the others around it. Once we're done we'll meet back at the first place. Don't get all the Ryba's shops confused. I'll go to the two I marked for me."
"Okay. Are we going today?"
"No. I'll show you around the island first today."

So that's what we did. As we rode our bikes, I showed her all around town. We rode the eight miles around the island, and we visited the fort. It was pretty fun. Maybe I should investigate being a tour guide!

Devon Warriner   ----------   Get Over it

Devon Warriner ---------- Get Over it

June 11th

Pink Bedroom

It takes Holly too long to wake up! She's still asleep! We have to eat, ride our bikes around, <u>and look for jobs</u>! Seriously! If she doesn't wake up soon I'm going to wake her up myself!

I'm so bored!!! No one's up yet. I'm going to look through the oldest pages in my notebook. Whoa! There's a prayer my Grandma wrote a long time ago.

"A Pot of Flowers
Greets me on the front porch
While I say
Good Morning to God
& Enjoy the blessings God gives me
God blesses me with the sweet songs of birds,
The hugs & smiles of grandchildren
And joy in my heart."

Now that was an almost exact copy. Okay. I'm bored. I'm going to go wake up Holly.

"Holls! Up please!" I called. Then I started a pillow fight, grabbing a pillow and slamming it on her back.

"Mmmm," was all Holly said in reply.

"Come on! We've got to get ready to job search! Let's go eat breakfast."

"Maddi?"

"Well, you're not much of a morning person. Let's try for an afternoon shift at wherever we work," I said as I hit her with my pillow again and then pulled hers out from under her.

"Fine! I'm getting up!" She got out of bed and headed for the door.

"Um. I think you should get dressed first," I suggested looking at her almost see-through white tank top. "My brother's in his girl-crazy stage."

"Oh. Good idea." She giggled, glancing down at her blue polka-dot bra. She changed into some denim jean shorts, and an orange sherbert colored shirt. "Okay, let's go." We headed downstairs to eat, finally.

"Hey. You're up," Mom greeted.

"I've been up for a *while*! I was waiting for this sleepyhead!" I said, jabbing a thumb at my friend. "Can we go downtown and look for jobs?"

"It's only ten o' clock, hon. Most places won't want anyone looking for jobs yet." I didn't know how true that was. Mom probably just wanted to keep us home longer. But I wasn't going to challenge it like that.

"Okay, more time to make sure Holly knows our meeting place! Can we go, please?"

"I guess…"

"Thanks, Mom! Holly, grab a muffin! We have to eat breakfast," I called out. We raced out the door, each grabbing two muffins and a water.

We rushed down the Grand Hill, going just slow enough that the police wouldn't stop us. "Okay, so I think we should meet in front of the fort instead. Do you remember how to get there?"

"Uh, Maddi, I can *see* it from basically anywhere on this street since it's on top of that hill! So we'll meet near the 'gazebo' tour thing on the sidewalk next to the fort?" Holly was talking about the Private Carriage gazebo on the sidewalk in front of the fort.

"Well, just checking. And yeah, we'll meet there. But since we've got time, let's just hang out."

We lounged on the fort 'lawn' for a while, watching people walking, biking, or cleaning their yachts in the harbor, and then we just window-shopped downtown.

"Hey, it's eleven-thirty. Let's go," Holly said suddenly, jumping up. As she headed for the fudge shops, I went up to the Gift Horse on my bike.

As I made my way to the counter, I noticed a guy looking through the shirts in the back of the store. He looked like he was my age.

"Excuse me," I said to the woman at the counter, "Is there any chance you're looking to hire anybody?" She was shaking her head before I even finished.

"No. But I think Murdick's and Joann's fudge shoppes are."

"Okay. Thank you for your help." I wandered through the store, staring at the guy. He had brown hair that looked silkier and softer than my thick, uncooperative hair. I hadn't realized, but I had gotten really close to him. I tripped over a basket full of stuffed animals. That he heard.

"Are you okay?" he asked, offering me his hand. I nodded. "Hey. I'm Ben."

"I'm Maddi," I replied, shaking his hand. He pulled me up. I was a little dizzy.

"Are you sure you're okay?"

"Yeah. I trip all the time. I've had worse," I blushed.

"Huh. You're clumsy," he said, pointing out the obvious. "So, why are you looking for a job?" he asked.

"Because I could use the money," I answered. Yeah, that was a pretty obvious answer, too.

"Are you moving here or what?"

"I'm just here for the rest of the month. Normally we're only here for a week, but my great-aunt gave us the cottage for almost a whole month. It's not really a cottage, it's about the same size as my house, but we call it a cottage anyway. Do you work here too?"

"Yes, I work here every summer. It's great, and you get used to the smell."

"I know what you mean. After a while, it even smells good," I said, both of us referring to the traffic on the island, which was only horses. "But maybe that's just my twisted mind," I giggled. Since when did I giggle after I said something? And talk so much? Ben started to say something, but I cut him off. "Well, I have to go." I turned to leave.

"Okay. See you around," Ben replied. "Oh! I think the Gate House is hiring!" he called as I walked out the door. I may have been paranoid, but I think he was staring after me.

I went to the Yankee Rebel Tavern next. They were hiring, and there were positions for both Holly and me. I told them I would come back with my friend tomorrow if she was interested, too. With that promise, I left for the fort yard.

"Hey. So, news. Murdick's is hiring, but they're only looking for one person. Same with Ryba's. Otherwise, no luck."

"Yankee Rebel Tavern is looking for two people. Interested so far?" I asked Holly.

"Sounds good. Is there a catch?"

"Wait, one person would have to be a lot like a janitor while the other's a waitress," I said, probably making it sound worse than it was.

"Ew. Okay, well, let's look more tomorrow," Holly suggested.

"Yeah, let's go to all the places left tomorrow, together. Hungry?" I questioned. "Cause I am. Let's go to lunch!"

"Hmm… I feel like pizza," Holly decided. So we went to my favorite Italian restaurant on the island, Sarducci Brothers.

"What are you staring at, Maddi?" Holly was glancing around frustrated, trying to figure out where I was looking. "Ooh! Are you looking at that hottie?" she exclaimed, glancing at the blonde in the corner.

"No. I'm just staring into space, trying to think." I answered. I didn't want to admit it, but I had been thinking about Ben. He was so cute!

"Well. That's not nearly as fun!" The pizza came sooner than I would have expected. We were super hungry and it disappeared quickly.

"Holly, are you done yet? 'Cause I feel like biking."

"Biking?…" She drew out the word, actually asking 'where?'.

"Around the island. The whole eight-ish miles, in the two hours before we have to be home. Come on! I bet we can do it twice!"

"Nah, no thanks. Take your cell, and I'll go home and tell them where you're going."

"Come on! I won't be able to go alone, if you get home without me, Mom will flip! We can do it just once."

"I never figured you for the sporty type. Why do you wanna go so bad?"

"Biking's my sport. All the others, I suck at. I just need some time to think."

"But how do you do that when you're riding a 'vehicle'?"

"Easy. But we can stop at that rocky beach about half-way around if you want."

"Okay," Holly finally agreed, standing up from the table.

Devon Warriner ---------- Get Over it

Devon Warriner ---------- Get Over it

June 11th

British Landing

Okay, first of all, I must sort out the jobs. I would most want to have a job at the old French Outpost. I know it doesn't have that name now, but I don't think the Grand Hotel should have bought it. I liked it best as the French Outpost.

Now, second, I guess we do still have freedom. I mean, we're seventeen, and smart. Of course we have lots of freedom. It's just that I always have to make sure Holly doesn't get lost, and we have to always be together. Plus there's a curfew. But that's to be expected. We have to be home for dinner.

Lastly, I really need to stop thinking about Ben. Yes, he's cute with those sparkling blue eyes, and his shiny brown hair. But I need to concentrate, and this is not the summer for a romance. I don't want one, especially with Bridget gone.

Oh my gosh! I've acted like Bridget hadn't existed for the last twenty-four hours. Like she wasn't my best friend in the world, like she's still alive at home. I feel so guilty! I need to act like my best friend just died. Because that's what really and truly happened. I need to make a resolution not to think like the world is all about me!

"Maddi, what are you writing?"

"Oh, I was just writing in my journal."

"Yeah, but why are you taking it everywhere?"

"I don't know! It's just thoughts and stuff. It seems natural to keep it around. Come on, let's leave for home," I finished.

"Okay. Do you know what's for dinner?" Holly questioned.

"I think Mom said pasties."

After that, it was a silent bike ride. Between the two of us, I mean. Other people and creatures were making plenty of noise. I was surprised; Holly was quiet and strangely un-hyper. It didn't fit right.

"Did I see a boy's name on that journal page?" Holly finally spoke as we pulled in the 'driveway' and it was a question I didn't want to answer. I knew this would come eventually.

"Yeah. I mentioned this guy I met in the Gift Horse. He was really obnoxious." I lied, crossing my fingers behind my back.

"Okay." Holly seemed wary, but she trusted me enough to accept that explanation. Now I really felt guilty. But what was I going to do? I didn't want to admit how self-absorbed I was! We headed inside to help set the table for dinner.

I was right, we had pasties for dinner. Oh, I miss Bridget's cooking. It was always so good! After we ate, we hung out for a while and then got caught up in a cut-throat game of dominoes with my family. The game went late into the night, and we were exhausted when we finally crawled into bed.

"Goodnight, Holly," I said.

"Night."

June 12th

Kitchen

    Oh my gosh! I woke up this morning and Holly was already up! It's completely shocking. But I did stay up later, after she was asleep, reading with a flashlight.

    I haven't even mentioned Aunt Annie, Uncle Chuck, and McKayla. They're getting here today. McKayla is almost five! She's so cute! Too bad I'll spend time at my job and with Holly, not watching that adorable little girl!

    Oops! Gotta go now. Holly and I are going to go pick them up. Once they get here, we'll go back through town and look for jobs.

"Hey!" I called to my relatives when I saw them get off the ferry. McKayla ran at me and hugged my legs. For such a little girl, she gives giant hugs. She tries to squeeze tightly, but her arms are still too short. "Oomph! Hey Mickie!"

"Hi," she answered a little shyly. Mickie was so cute! Her thin brunette bob bounced as she jumped, and her eyes were so pretty. Blue-gray, and green near the pupil. And yeah, she'll let me call her Mickie, but no one else can. It's the same with her mother and me. Only Aunt Annie can call me anything besides Maddi.

"Okay, so Holly, this is my Aunt Annie, Uncle Chuck, and my cousin Mickie." I gestured to each of them as I said their name.

"Hey Mickie. As in the mouse?" Holly asked.

"No. If I went by mouses, I'd be Minnie," McKayla replied.

"You mean mice, Mick," I corrected.

"Okay," she agreed. Mickie's so smart for a four year-old! I don't know how her parents did it.

"You ready to go, McKayla?" Uncle Chuck asked. His blue-gray eyes looked tired, while Mickie's were eager.

"Yeah." She hopped in the trailer hitched to her dad's bike.

"Well, then let's go," suggested my aunt. She looked tired, too. There were bags under her green eyes. I wondered if Mickie had kept them up last night. So we all headed for the Grand Hill and Dufina.

"We're going to go back downtown now, so..." Holly drifted off.

"Okay, we get it. See you later, Mouse!" Mickie called to us.

"Who's Mouse?" Holly asked.

"You. Because you asked her the Mickey question. And she hates that question. But she'll probably still let you call her Mickie," I said. "Ooh. Turn here."

"Why?"

"Because we're going to take the way that goes in front of the Grand Hotel. It's the prettiest way to get to town," I explained. "There is a really great bluff to look out over the water and the bridge, and the cottages along the street are amazing!"

"Okay!" Holly exclaimed. After that, we lapsed back into silence. But it wasn't uncomfortable. At least, not for Holly. I was thinking about how Bridget never rode in front of the Grand. I guess that was a missed opportunity.

"Hey!" someone called in the slight distance. Thinking he couldn't possibly be talking to us, we kept biking. But he called again, so we stopped. He was running toward us.

I started to say something, but I trailed off. There, in front of us, stood Ben. "Oh. Hi."

"Hi," he replied.

"Maddi, I'm going to get a start on the Gate House. Meet you down there." Holly subtly excused herself. Well, subtle in her book. I thought it was rather obvious.

"I thought I recognized you. No one else I've seen has hair that color, or a bike that orange." Ben said smoothly. Despite the fact I didn't want to do this, I blushed.

"Really? Exactly what color is my hair?" I questioned curiously. At this point, I figured he was flirting, so I wanted to know what he'd say. And I was never sure that I liked my hair color. I hated wearing oranges and reds, because I thought they looked bad with my hair. Too bad one of my school's colors was red.

"Oh, strawberry-chestnut," he answered, reaching out to play with my hair. "And not many people I know have hazel eyes. They're all brown-eyed or blue."

"What do you want?" I asked. I pulled away from him quickly, and I had become very rude. It was like I expected him to know I didn't want him to talk to me like that. With the sound of that affection. It just didn't feel right to me this summer.

"Oh, I wanted to ask you if you'd want to go to dinner with me," he persisted.

Even though my brain said no, my heart said yes, and my heart won the fight. "Yes," I said, shocked at what I had blurted.

"Okay. Meet me at…" For the first time, he was uncertain.

"I like Mary's Bistro and Yankee Rebel Tavern." I tried to help, since I couldn't take it back.

"Mary's Bistro then. At six?"

"Um… Actually, lunch is better. Noon?"

"That's fine. Tomorrow, then."

"Okay. I have to go now," I managed to say.

"I know. See you later." He turned to go back on the porch, but he kept watching me. His "I know" really aggravated me. I biked the rest of the way down the hill to the Gate House.

"Two equal spots open for the same shift," Holly informed me.

"That's awesome." I tried, but I sounded unenthusiastic.

"So, who was *that?*" Holly asked, punctuating the word "that" like a balloon with a needle.

"Nobody. And you know, I really don't like Fred's, and bike rental stores only ever have two employees at a time, and sucky bikes. I don't want to get blamed for any problems customers have with their bikes. Let's try for this one," I said, lying. I *did* like Fred's. They gave the most ice cream in a cone, usually, and it tasted good. The bike places had older bikes, but they weren't sucky. At least, most of them weren't. But Holly wasn't going to forget this so easily.

"So do you like him?" she continued. "That was a long speech for a distraction tactic."

"No. I don't," I lied.

"Okay." 'Confused' was written all over her face. We headed inside and an employee handed us applications. The manager said he'd review them and get back to us. I felt my stomach twist and willed it to go away. But the only way it would go away was knowing if we were hired or not.

"Let's stay in town for a while, just in case, okay?"

"Fine. Let's go hang out… somewhere," Holly suggested, her mind turning a blank.

"How about the 'fort yard'?"

"Okay. Let's go."

Devon Warriner   ----------   Get Over it

June 12th

Pink Bedroom

It's official. We have jobs at the Gate House. Our shift is 11:00 AM to 5:00 PM. We start the day after tomorrow, which is sad, because if we started tomorrow, I could avoid lunch with Ben.

Which reminds me. Why did I say yes?! I wanted to say no, but I said yes. How does that make sense?! It doesn't! And how am I going to get away from Holly and my family? Oooh! I'll tell Holly we'll go shopping and then meet in an hour or so. Yeah, that works. So we'll have to leave at quarter to noon, about.

Oh. Have to go to bed now!

"Hey. It's eleven o'clock!" Holly said.

"Huh?"

"You're not the best morning person either, Maddi," she remarked.

"Fine, I'm up. What?" I sat up.

"Well, our shift starts at this time tomorrow, so shouldn't we at least get up at ten?"

"Earlier than that. We have to eat lunch before we go," I thought aloud.

"Oh. So, after we eat breakfast, want to go shopping?" Holly suggested.

"Sure. Let's meet up outside Doud's Grocery at one," I agreed.

"Well, I meant together, but that's fine too," she replied. I exhaled in relief. We ate pretty quickly, and then walked downtown.

"Gross! That's just nasty!" Holly exclaimed when we passed some fresh, unavoidable horse poop on Market Street.

"But you can't stop them. You sound like a first timer."

"I practically am! It's been seven years since I was last here," she joked.

"Okay. Let's go down this side road," I suggested.

"I want to go into Monkey Business," Holly said when we got to the main street.

"Hey, Holls, I've been up here often enough to not exactly want to do an hour of shopping, so I'm going to eat lunch down here too," I informed her.

"Fine. I'm going to eat lunch at the cottage. I want to *shop*!" she replied. I laughed a little. She reminded me a little of this character in a book that we were crazy about a year ago. It was still one of my favorite books, but I wasn't obsessed anymore. I walked at what I guessed was a normal pace until she walked into Monkey Business.

* * *

"Hey," Ben said to me as I met him outside Mary's. "Deck or inside?"

"I've never eaten inside. But I feel like eating on the deck."

"Okay." We walked inside. "Two for the deck, please."

"It's a different menu," the host said quickly in a different accent. He talked too fast for me to be able to figure out where he was from.

"That's what we want," Ben told him. So he led us to the deck, where another person led us to a table. Before Ben said anything else after we were seated, our waitress came up to us.

"Hello. My name is Tori. I'll be your server. What can I get you to drink?" she asked.

"I'll have a…" I paused, indecisive.

"Coke, please," Ben interrupted. A little rude, but I probably would have taken a while.

"Yeah, I'll have the same," I said. "So…"

"So who are your friends?" Ben asked right away.

"Well, Holly is one. You saw her with me near the Grand Hotel. I have another friend named Emily, and my best friend is Bridget." I corrected myself in my head – was.

"What are they like?"

"Holly's normally hyper. Well, just bubbly. Emily is really thoughtful, blonde- she acts like it a lot, and I think, probably one of the nicest of my…"

"Your friends are mean?" he interrupted again. Okay, that was getting a little irritating.

"No. Just, they still 'burn' all of us. Holly doesn't do it as much, but I think I've only seen Emily burn someone three times in all the time I've known her."

"What about Bridget?" I really didn't want to answer this one.

"She's… hard to describe," I said simply.

"Okay." For once he didn't tack on a question right away, so I jumped in.

"What about your friends?"

"Well, my closest friends are Josh and Zack, and they can be really obnoxious sometimes."

"Then why…" I started.

"You don't get it. They're obnoxious, but I love 'em." He paused for a few seconds.

"Are you ready to order?" the waitress reappeared and asked.

"Cheeseburger, please. Medium to well done," I ordered.

"What kind of cheese? We have…"

"Oh. Cheddar," I offered.

"I'll have a hot dog." I looked at him funny.

"What, do you have to order cheap or something?" I remembered that the hot dog was the cheapest meal on the menu. "You could have told me…" I said, staring after the waitress as she walked away.

"Hey, I just wanted a hot dog. So, do you go to church?"

"Yeah, do you?" I wondered why he asked this question.

"Yup." His lips popped on the p. "Where do you go?"

"Saint Mary's."

"Sorry, that's not what I meant. What kind of church?"

"Oh. Catholic."

"I'm Methodist, and I'm very involved in my church. You know, when I was little, my mom made a big deal about how I have to marry a Christian." There was an awkward silence. "I don't mean that! When parents bug you that much, things tend to stick just a little. My mom will ask if you're a Christian when I get home, and I'd rather not say 'I don't know!' I don't want to get into that again. Plus I was curious." It was quiet between us for a couple minutes. I stared at the waterfront for a minute. "So, did you get a job?"

"What?" I said, startled. I hadn't told him… "Oh." I realized he had been in the Gift Horse when I was looking for a job. "Yeah. Holly and

I got jobs at the Gate House, eleven AM to five PM." Then I burst out laughing.

"What?" he asked a little indignant, thinking I was laughing at him.

"Nothing. I just thought of something," I managed to say as I stopped laughing. If I worked 11:00 AM to 5:00 PM, and dinner was between 5:00 and 6:00, I couldn't really go on dates with him.

"Okay... So if you work then, how can we go out again?" he asked.

"I don't know," I replied. Really, I knew that he could come hang out in my section at a table as long as he ordered something, but I didn't want him to figure that out. That would give things away to Holly, not to mention that I didn't really want a second date. All of a sudden, he smiled. I hoped this was not because he figured that out.

"Why are you smiling?" I questioned warily.

"No reason," he said swiftly. Finally, after what seemed like a long time, the waitress brought out our food.

"Thanks," I said to her. She thought I meant for the food. I really meant for the distraction. There was a silence while we ate. Apparently Ben didn't like silences, because he started talking again.

"So you're not a salad girl?" he asked.

"No. I'm not a fan of eating just salad for any meal. Plus, was there even salad on that menu?" I replied.

"I doubt it. Everything out here was made on the grill."

"My turn to ask questions," I said. "Where do you go to school?"

"I went to school on the island." When I heard this, so many questions assailed my brain that it took a few seconds for me to grasp just one.

"You live here?" I asked. Ben nodded. "Cool!"

"Yeah, I like it here," Ben answered.

"How old are you? I mean like, did you just graduate or did you drop out?" I had noticed he used the word "went," as in past tense.

"I would never drop out. I'm eighteen, and I just graduated," he replied.

"Oh. So… where are you going to college?"

"I don't know."

"But don't you normally have to let them know earlier than this?"

"Yes, but I got an extension on that deadline."

"Oh." I didn't want to push that any farther. I decided that the simplest obvious questions were safe. "What's your favorite… color?"

"I don't have one. You?"

"Green." The questions went on while we ate, so we took a while. "Oh my gosh! It's twelve-forty five. I have to walk down to Doud's Market to meet Holly!"

"Okay," Ben replied. I looked at the table. Apparently Ben had already paid.

"About twenty minutes." I heard from his phone.

"What did you just do?" I questioned nervously.

"I got a taxi for you. It'll pick you up in front of Doud's."

"Oh. I have to go now." I got up to leave. Ben stood up too. I turned around to look at him.

"I'm coming with you."

"You can't!" I exclaimed, panicked.

Surprised, he asked, "Why not?" I blushed.

"I didn't tell Holly," I admitted reluctantly.

"Fine. I'll show up after you." Thinking that was the best offer I could get, I agreed. I ran to Doud's, since it was so far away.

"Hey, Holly," I said, breathing hard. "I called a taxi. Let's wait and take it."

"Okay." We were quiet for a minute.

"So what did you get?" I prompted. Normally she would have shown me as soon as I got there. As she was showing me her shirt from Monkey Business, I saw Ben show up out of the corner of my eye.

"Annex?" a taxi driver asked.

"That's us," I said. "Dufina Cottage," I added to make sure.

"And me," Ben added. I had to stop and think for a second. How did he know where we were staying in the first place? I guess he saw us in front of the Grand Hotel… maybe he assumed we lived in the Annex, since part of it was just past the Grand Hotel. Good thing he got it right! We hopped onto the taxi, and it was a pretty quiet ride. I just sat on the bench listening to the sound the horses' hooves made. Clip-clop, clip-clop.

"Dufina?" The taxi driver spoke again.

"Yeah, for two of us," I answered. *Please don't try to get off with us!* I silently begged.

"$11.50, then, please," she said.

"Maddi, I'm going inside. I'll pay you back," Holly told me. I pulled out my wallet.

"I'm not letting you pay!" Ben exclaimed. "There's their fare, I'll finish paying when I'm dropped off," he added to the driver.

"Okay then, Ben. Bye." I started to step off.

"Wait a second, Maddi!" he almost yelled. I really hope Holly wasn't listening. He wasn't supposed to know my name. Well, not with what Holly knew.

"What?" I turned around, and he was looking at me a little strangely. I didn't know what that expression meant. But soon I found out, because his lips were against mine. It was the shortest kiss I've ever had (Of course, I only had one boyfriend before). But it left me dizzy and made my heart race. "Okay. Bye then," I said. It didn't make any sense to be dizzy after only a couple-seconds kiss. But I was. It was an odd feeling. I wavered a little on the path up to the back of the house. I might have looked like I was drunk, so I really hoped everyone was on the front porch on the other side of the house, or at least not in the rooms I was going to walk through.

"So…" Holly said as I walked into our room. She dragged out the word, like she knew something. Oh, no!

"So… what?" I acted cool and collected, which I thought was pretty believable.

"So who was that you were kissing?" she continued. I looked at her. Her face was too bright for me to think I could get out of this.

"You know that guy I said was obnoxious who I met in the Gift Horse?" Holly nodded, so I kept going. "Well, he asked me out after you 'subtly' excused yourself to the Gate House," I said, looking at her to see what she would do. She opened her mouth to protest something, and assuming it was the air quotes I did when I said "subtly", I started first. "Yes, I fully mean the air quotes I put around subtly. And today was our date."

"So how was it?"

"I actually kind of enjoyed it. But that makes me feel guilty because of Bridget," I started.

"Hey! Stop that!" Holly interrupted. "So your best friend isn't here. That doesn't mean you can't have any fun," she shouted curtly.

"I don't know," I hesitated. But I have to admit, it sounded right. Like, something clicked in my brain, telling me something was right. "You can't tell anyone. Especially my family. Especially especially my aunt."

"What about Emily?"

"Um… okay, she'll find out no matter what."

"Now why 'especially especially' your aunt?"

"'Cause she likes romance, and she's a bit of a gossip."

"Okay." Holly accepted this explanation like she accepted all the lies about Ben. Did she not believe me? "Do you mind if I call Emily now?"

"No," I replied.

June 14th

Pink Bedroom

Emily is excited that I have a boyfriend- sort of. I guess that's not really his "title" yet, but one date is more than I've had in a long time. She said that she didn't think I'd be dating again for a long time, since... Well. Anyway. Boyfriend. That word makes me nervous. But Holly's right. Fun is good. Plus, there are no cars on this island.

Our jobs start today. In fact, they start in roughly two hours. I admit, I am a little nervous. But it's waitressing. We'll get good tips.

Ooh! Mickie's up! I'm going to go play with that girl!

"Hey Mickie. Morning."

"Hi, Maddi," Mickie walked to the kitchen. I followed her and watched as she poured cereal into a bowl she got by hoisting herself onto the counter.

"So what are you doing today?" I asked.

"I don't know. Probably biking somewhere," she replied. "What are you doing?"

"Leaving for my job at approximately ten-thirty. I start at eleven, but I have to get there early."

"Oh. Where do you work?" Mickie looked a little disappointed and like she didn't want to be left behind. Did she seriously look up to me that much?

"The Gate House. My shift ends at five," I told my cousin. Just then, my aunt walked in.

"Mommy, can we eat at the Gate House today?"

"Why, sweetie?" Aunt Annie prodded.

"Because Maddi works there!" Mickie informed her.

Aunt Annie shot me a surprised look before she hugged her daughter and said "Maybe, McKayla." I left the kitchen to go read in my bed while I waited for Holly to shower and get ready. Annie appeared in the doorway.

"You got a job at the *Gate House* even though you're here for less than a month?" she exclaimed.

"Of course," Holly interrupted, walking in as she was towel-drying her hair.

"Yeah, they let us interview right away and then gave us the job."

"Although, they thought at first that we wanted to be cooks," Holly added.

"They did?" I didn't know this before.

"Yeah, 'cause the guy I was asking was Mexican," Holly said to me.

"Wow. One of the seventeen Mackinac Island Mexican workers works at the Gate House," I mumbled.

"Actually, like five of them do. How do you know there's only seventeen Mexican workers?"

"I heard it somewhere. No, wait, that was from last year. The Saint Anne's deacon announced it, along with where most of the seasonal workers come from. Oops. Oh, I'm going to stay in town today after work so I can go to church. Want to come?" I added, so as not to be impolite.

"No, I'll just window shop."

"Okay. Mass will be over around six-thirty. Meet me outside the church?"

"Where's the church again?" Holly questioned.

"It's past the fort on the main road. It has a really tall steeple. Just ride past the fort until you see it, okay?"

"Yeah, I got it now," Holly replied.

"You two girls have fun today. See you at dinner," Aunt Annie said as she left the room.

"Ten o' clock. It's early, but maybe we should eat a snack?" Holly asked.

"Yeah, sure," I agreed. Holly had a turkey sandwich, while I just had peanut butter and jelly. I didn't feel like eating any meat. We were pretty quiet while we ate, mostly because Mickie had come in and was telling us a story about the tooth fairy that she obviously made up.

"And the Tooth Fairy's castle is made up of a whole bunch of teeth! Santa likes to visit her there because she cleans them so much, they're so pretty that they shine…" We never got to hear what Santa does at the Tooth Fairy's home, because I had to interrupt Mickie.

"Oh. Would you look at the time! We have three minutes! We have to go get ready to go. See you, Mick!" I said.

"Bye!" Holly and I went outside, put our helmets on, and hopped on our bikes and left.

"Good morning, ladies," the manager greeted us. "Why are you not in uniform?"

"We never got a uniform," Holly replied. I was worried now. We were supposed to get a uniform?

"Oh. Well," he said, dismayed even more. He started walking through the restaurant, searching. "Ah. Here we are. Sizes?"

"Medium for shirts, ten for pants," I replied shyly. He handed me the items of clothing.

"Same, please," Holly added.

"I would invest in some khaki skirts or pants and buy another shirt if I were you," Mr. Poe suggested.

"You're the same sizes as me?" I asked when we were in the bathroom to change. Good thing Holly brought a bag.

"Yeah. You didn't know that?" she replied.

"Nope." I stared at my reflection in the mirror. That shade of orange didn't look good on me. Oh well. The khaki skirt was okay, though. I was assigned a section outside, and Holly was a hostess because they were short one.

"Hello. Would you like to eat outside or in?" I heard Holly ask a couple. Obviously they said out, because she was leading them towards my section.

"My name is Maddi, and I'll be your server today. What can I get you to drink?" I asked a couple minutes after they were seated. They both hesitated. *"Too early, too early..."* I said in my head. They finally decided, so I left to get their drinks. When I came back, two more groups were seated. I repeated my little speech, and after maybe eight minutes, all nine of my customers were happy. I went over to Holly.

"How long do I wait before going over to ask what they want?" I questioned.

"Well, that couple is waving you over, so I'd say now," Holly suggested. I looked up. Sure enough, the first couple was staring at me impatiently. After the first few times of doing this, I gained confidence and I discovered I was good at it, and it wasn't so hard. Of course, we didn't really hit any busy times until almost 1:00 PM. I noticed my section was almost full.

"Is there space for us in Maddi's section?" I heard my aunt ask over at the hostess stand. Well, that was it, completely full. I started making the rounds, first to a couple, then a family a four, a group of six, and a family of three. I came to a table that had just one person at it. Without even looking at him, I launched into my introduction.

"Hi, I'm Maddi..."

"I know."

"I'll be your server today..."

"That would be why I'm sitting in your section."

"What would you like to drink?" I finally finished.

"Okay, seriously Maddi, how can I distract you from that speech?" Ben teased.

"It doesn't matter now. I finished it," I said. "Now what would you like to drink?"

"Okay, fine, Coke."

"Good, I have to go now." I walked over to my relatives' table. Wait. Ben was here. Aunt Annie was here. This was not a good situation.

"Hey Madster! I'll have a Diet Coke, Uncle Chuck will have the same, and... Mickie?" Aunt Annie prompted her daughter.

"McKayla," Mickie corrected.

"Okay, are you trying to imitate Uncle Jack?" I interrupted. My youngest uncle seemed slightly insane, he called some of my family members nicknames like "Ryanator" and backwards names like "Werdna," for Andrew, adding on "bellyslammer". He often calls my brother names like "Luke-a-licious" and "Luke-a-lay-lee." We all thought he'd named the Wendy's Baconator.

"No," she replied.

"Um... milk please," Mickie said at the same time.

"Okay, I'm doing my job now." I made the rounds, delivering the drinks. When I came to Ben's table, I had to ask a favor.

"Ben, would you please not flirt with me until my aunt leaves? I don't want her to know. Please?" I begged.

"Who said I would hit on you in the first place?" he replied with a smile. I just looked at him. "Okay," he finally agreed.

"Thank you. Oh, and by the way, it's a little late for that comment. You hit on me at the Grand Hotel," I smirked.

It was a pretty busy two hours, but things started winding down around three o'clock in the afternoon. My relatives left about fifteen minutes before then. There were still some people eating, but most of them were inside. I went up to the manager.

"Can I take a break?"

"I guess. Fifteen, starting now," he replied. I went out to sit with Ben.

"So how's your first day so far?" he asked.

"Uh..." I said. I didn't know what to say. "Confusing. Busy. And not exactly helpful that you're here."

"That's hurtful, Maddi." Ben pouted, making me smile. Which was probably the point.

"It shouldn't be. You just claim more of my attention than anyone else."

"Okay, fine. Do you want me to leave, then?"

"I don't know, Ben," I said, getting a little frustrated, just like Ben was. "I still have two more hours until my shift's over. But then I'm going to church."

"Why?"

"Because I don't feel like going to Mass at nine o' clock tomorrow, and my shift starts at eleven. It'll be easier to go tonight."

"Okay, I'll leave, then," Ben said. He leaned in to kiss me quickly. Then he left. "Bye, Maddi."

"Bye," I whispered.

"I saw that," the manager said. "Did you read the entire employee handbook?"

"I think so."

"How many rules were there?" he asked.

"Thirty-seven," I replied. To me, that many rules seemed excessive.

"Ah. You missed the last rule on the back of the page. 'No public displays of affection'. But since you didn't know, this is a warning," he informed me. Wow. Mr. Poe was *creepy*.

The rest of my shift was very non-busy, because not many tourists eat lunch that late, or dinner that early. In almost no time, new people showed up for their shift. We were released after a good day. Finally!

Devon Warriner   ----------   Get Over it

June 14th
Outside Ste. Anne's

    Wow! The first day of work was strange. Really busy at first, I hope tomorrow is the same without the Ben/Aunt Annie drama.

    I knew it! He was smiling on our date after I told him when I work! I knew he had figured it out! Oh please, I hope he doesn't show up tomorrow.

    Oh! Speaking of which, the manager Mr. Poe, is creepy. Ooh! Like an Edgar Allen Poe story. He was creepy and confusing. Excessively creepy and confusing. He's the only person I don't like at the Gate House so far.

    Hey, Holly's here, I'm going to go now.

"Hey Holls!" I shouted at my friend.

"Hey, so how was church?" she asked, anxiously glancing at Ste. Anne's like they were going to kidnap her.

"I liked that priest. He talks fast, but he gives great homilies."

"Huh? Isn't he there every year?"

"No. He was a guest from," I paused, thinking back to an hour ago, "somewhere in Illinois. And a homily is what the priest talks about after reading the Gospel." I stopped to look at Holly. She still looked confused, so I explained more. "The Gospel is the third reading when everybody stands," I breathed. Not looking up, I thought *"If she doesn't understand that, I don't know what to do. That's the simplest terms I can come up with."* Comprehension was finally dawning on Holly. She was so easy to read.

"Okay, so anyway, I wanted to ask you something random," Holly said as we finally mounted our bikes.

"Shoot."

"Have you ever noticed how every song you hear normally talks about love?"

"Wow, that is kind of random. Yeah, I guess. It's just normal to me. Why?"

"Oh, I was just listening to my iPod, and every song did..."

"Okay, I'm not talking on the way up that hill, I'll meet you at the top," I stated, pushing my pedals harder without waiting for a reply. I knew it was a little rude, but I think I knew exactly what she was going to say. I made it up the hill in a couple minutes. Draining my water bottle, I waited for Holly.

"So, back to my hidden meaning comment. The world revolves around romance, you should have some," Holly panted, out of breath.

"Holly, stop it. Seriously. I'm dating Ben, what else do you want us to do? I'm not doing anything more than dating," I said, getting a little mad, but wanting to cry at the same time.

"I definitely didn't mean *that!* I'm just still trying to convince you it's okay to date."

"Uh... I am. Give it up!" I exclaimed, frustrated. "Come on, let's go." I started to pedal again. Holly didn't answer, but just went with me.

"So how was your first day of work?" Mom asked when we got home.

"Busy. Confusing," I replied.

"You forgot fun!" Holly added.

"No, I didn't. It wasn't that fun," I said. Pausing, I glanced at my mom. She started to say something, but I cut her off. "I'm not quitting. The job pays pretty good money with tips, and I'd give it a second chance no matter what."

"Well, that's a good idea," Mom said, impressed. She had a slight triumphant look on her face, probably because I didn't interrupt her again. Childish, I know. Holly and I headed upstairs to dump our stuff. I was glad I had changed before church, because it seemed really hot.

"Why wasn't it fun?" Holly questioned.

"Can't you guess?" I answered.

"Yeah, but..." She trailed off.

"Fine," I said, shutting the door. "Ben *and* Aunt Annie were both there and making me feel stressed."

"Okay, but why don't you just tell your family?"

"'Cause..."

"I mean, they won't ground you or anything..."

"Just, I'll tell them when it's the right time, okay?" I sighed.

"Okay. I'm starved! Let's go get dinner," Holly said, walking to the door. I spaced as we walked into the kitchen. Mom was making spaghetti and meatballs. I love her meatballs! Grandma's and Aunt Annie's too. Of course, all the recipes are the same...

"...okay. You guys helped last night," I heard my mom say to Holly as I came back to earth. "You okay there, Maddi?"

"Yeah, Mom, I'm fine. I just spaced for a little."

"Well, Maddi, your Mom's getting Luke to set the table today, so we're free for a while," Holly told me. Instead of replying, I walked into the family room and started helping on the puzzle. The annual puzzle. We didn't finish it last year. "Seriously, Maddi, are you okay?"

"Yes! I guess my lack of sleep finally caught up to me," I snapped as I fit a piece into the border. "Ha!"

"Okay, but you need to space back in, it's almost dinnertime." My friend sifted through the box full of pieces, searching.

June 14th

Family Room

I just realized something a couple minutes ago. I served this African-American woman earlier who looked kind of familiar... Her hair was dyed white-blonde, and hung straight down. She needed to dye the roots again. But anyway, her eye had this tick. Maybe I'm just going insane! But I really don't think I am. She was wearing a spring green spaghetti-strap tank top, and white Capri's.

Maddi...

Huh?!?!?!?!

"Maddi, are you okay? I'm serious, you've been weird since we got home!" Holly exclaimed. Oh. I had started writing what she said in my journal. "Maddi!"

"Huh?" I asked, glancing at my journal and closing it. "Oh. Yeah. I guess. Sorry that I'm so spaced."

"Guess what! The parade's tomorrow!" Mickie shouted.

"Are you working tomorrow?" Aunt Annie asked as she walked in the room.

"Yeah. I just have Wednesday's off."

"Odd time," she remarked, hugging her enthusiastic daughter.

"Well…"

"Anyway, dinner's ready."

"So these magic binonlars…"

"Binoculars, Mickie," Holly corrected, beating everyone to it.

"Right. They'll take you wherever you want to go…" Mickie was narrating another story as we ate.

"Honey, why don't you eat? You don't have to entertain us," Mickie's mother suggested, clearly implying one of us had to. I was betting she meant me. "So, do you girls think any of the guys you've seen are cute?"

"Not really. But there was this blond guy. Normally I don't go for blonds, but his haircut was cute, and his face was a little baby-ish, though grown up," Holly answered quickly, not wanting to shoulder the weight. She obviously thought a quick answer and explanation meant that Annie wouldn't go after her. But I knew my aunt better.

"No," I answered simply, refusing the burden. Aunt Annie was hesitant. Probably debating whether to challenge me or push Holly. She picked Holly. Ooh! Lucky Holls!

June 15th

Back Porch

Today is the Lilac Parade. It won't even be going by us because we're not on the main street. Oh, well, I guess I'll just get Mickie to describe it. Dangerous, I know, but...

I know that I know that lady from somewhere!

I give up! It's not good to obsess over this, and I can't figure it out... So I give up.

"Hey Maddi. Are you better today?" Holly asked sleepily. I looked up from my notebook. Her hair was definitely in need of washing, and she was dressed in her old tie-dye shirt and athletic shorts.

"I guess. Hey. Whatever happened to wearing nightgowns to bed?" I asked curiously. Holly used to try to wear pajama shorts or pants to bed, but she would wake up without any, having kicked them off when she was sleeping. So she had switched to wearing nightgowns instead.

"I outgrew kicking off the shorts."

"Oh. That's good," I said.

"I'm going to go wash my hair. See you later."

"Yeah, okay." Holly left me sitting alone on the porch. I sat staring at the yard. The beautiful lilacs were already dying, and the mini-daisies growing in the lawn were already open again. It was beautiful, even with the brown patches on the purple lilac flowers, and the small patches of dead grass. It was peaceful.

As much as I didn't want to, I had to get up and eat. And then go to work after that. Holly kept me going when all I wanted to do was go home. Only my second day of work, but it already seemed tedious. This was going to be a long day.

"Maddi, Ben's here," Holly said, pointing to the entrance. I went up to him, smiling. Holly gave me a thumbs-up when she went up to Mr. Poe. I turned back to Ben and kissed him, grabbed his hand, and brought him to a table.

"This day has been so boring," I remarked.

"So I'm your entertainment?" he asked, smiling.

"Yeah."

"Okay. I'm good with that. I thought public-displays-of-affection would get you fired, though."

"Well, Holly's distracting Creepy, and I was hoping you would show up today. I've been waiting this whole time!"

"You mean for five hours?"

"Yeah."

"So, I realized something last night. I don't even have your phone number," Ben said.

"Oh." I pulled out my pen and a napkin and wrote the ten-digit number on it. "Now you do."

"Okay. Thanks," he said, pulling out his cell phone to program my number. "By the way, I'd like a Coke."

"I know that. It's what you always order. But okay, I'll do my job," I replied, acting sad.

"Hey, I just don't want you to get fired."

"I know you care. So I'll go do my job." I got all my customers content quickly, so I brought Ben his Coke. "So do you want anything else?" I asked him.

"Nope."

"Okay..." I said, trailing off, at a loss for what to say.

"Miss...?" Someone else was calling me to his table.

"Gotta go," I said to Ben. "What would you like?" I asked the man at the next table over. His dark hair was thinning, he had brown eyes, and a sharp nose. His blue shirt looked uncomfortable because it was dark, and this was the warmest day I've experienced on Mackinac.

"Could I have a refill," he asked, pointing to his glass, "and a dessert menu?"

"Sure." I went to fetch the things he wanted, and passed Holly. She was staring with narrowed eyes at something behind me.

"Turn around," she said, pointing with her eyes. I followed her glare. One of the waitresses had stopped by Ben's table and was very obviously flirting with him. She was the girl with the strawberry-blond curly hair. I was pretty sure her name was Sara. My stomach flipped as the sudden jealousy clawed at it and I was scared that he would start flirting back. I wanted to run over there and rip her pretty hair out, as well as tell her that Ben was taken. Normally I wouldn't be worried, I would have faith in my guy to tell her he was into someone else. But our first date was only two days ago, and I just wasn't sure what he thought yet. My stomach turned more as I watched them, and every second I fought the urge to hurt her. Then a second later she stormed angrily away, and Ben laughed to himself. I sighed in relief. I barely remembered that I had an order to get. I walked to Ben's table, breathing slowly to calm myself down more.

"So did you like that girl?" I teased Ben, getting over the jealousy and scary feelings fast.

"Yeah," he answered with a smile.

"Enough to make her storm off? Does that mean you don't like me?"

"Yeah, I kiss all the girls I don't like and make the ones I do like angry. That makes total sense, Maddi," He said sarcastically, with a little anger in his voice.

"Hey, I wasn't being serious yet!" I exclaimed, wondering how that made him mad so fast. "Oh. I guess I better get that guy's order, now that I remember it," I said, glancing over Ben's shoulder to Dessert Menu Guy.

I tried to stay at Ben's table as much as possible. Surprisingly, it was easy. Mr. Poe had another waitress cornered, giving a lecture, and my other customers were indecisive. When I wasn't at Ben's table, I found myself glancing his way often. He smiled at me, and the butterflies flew around my stomach. Too soon Ben paid for his Coke and left, but not before squeezing my hand. My stomach twisted yet again when he did that. By that time there was only twenty minutes until my shift was over.

"Are you going straight home this time?" Holly asked when I passed her on the way to put the money in the register.

"Yeah. I only go to church after work on Saturdays."

"I knew that. But I thought you might want to do something else."

"Nope." I popped my lips on the 'p'. Which reminded me of Ben.

"Okay.

June 15th

Pink Bedroom

    Mickie's going to tell me about the Lilac Parade in a couple minutes. That should be fun. I'm really wondering if she'll make anything up. Oh. I really shouldn't be wondering. I know she'll make <u>something</u> up!

    I wonder what made Ben mad so fast. All I remember is saying "Enough to make her storm off? Does that mean you don't like me?" in a teasing voice. Hey, if he got mad at me for saying that, does it mean he likes me a lot?! Oh, does he love me?! Wait. We've only had our first date. And that was two days ago. He probably doesn't love me. Yet. But he does like me if he got mad at me for teasing him about "not liking me!"

"The horses were dressed up! Their tails were braided and there was sparkly stuff in their..." Mickie hesitated in her tale. "What is it called on their neck?"

"The mane," I answered.

"Yeah! There was sparkly stuff in their manes. They were pretty! And there was this Girl Scout troop in the parade too! Aren't you a girl scout?"

"Yeah... Not many people my age are now."

"What color is your uniform?"

"Tan."

"Oh. They were wearing green. What are they?"

"They're juniors, then."

"So many people were in costume or dressed up! There were four girls with really pretty dresses on sitting in a carriage, waving. They all had white... what are they called?"

"What are what called?" I asked.

"The thing that goes across your chest," Mickie said, demonstrating where they were.

"Oh. Sashes," I answered.

"Yeah! All four of them had white sashes on that said different things. But I don't know what they said. I couldn't read them and Mom and Dad wouldn't read them for me." Mickie lay down on Holly's bed. We were in the pink bedroom, talking about the parade. Holly was actually sitting next to me, but she wasn't really talking.

"Mickie, I have to go to the bathroom. Tell Holly all this stuff!" I suggested, getting up.

"Okay. Um... There were those things that are like bags with a lot of sticks coming out of them that make music. You know, the ones Maddi's dad hates?" Mickie said as I left the room.

"Bagpipes?" Holly asked.

"Yeah." Mickie's voice drifted through the door. I walked into the bathroom and closed the door, then stared at myself in the mirror that wasn't above the sink. Old bathrooms. I sighed. I didn't know what to do.

I didn't have to go to the bathroom, I was just trying to get Holly included in the conversation. I sat on the lip of the clawfoot tub for a couple minutes. When I thought I had taken long enough, I left the bathroom.

"You took a while," Holly remarked when I came back to our room.

"Yeah, I agree with Mouse," Mickie said. Huh. I guess I was gone longer than I thought.

"Anyway... What else, Mickie?"

"Um..." she stalled. I could almost see the gears in her head turning, trying to make up a story. Just then, my phone rang.

"Sorry, Mickie." I looked at the number. Who the heck was that? Well, one way to find out. "Hello?" I asked, almost positive I knew who it was.

"Hi, Maddi," I heard someone say. I shot a glance at Holly, pleading her to get Mickie out of here. She seemed confused at first, but then she understood.

"Come on, Mick. Let's go play a game," she suggested. Mickie wasn't protesting not being called McKayla. Ha! Good. They left, and I waited.

"Uh... Hello?" Ben asked.

"Hi. Sorry, Mickie was in the room."

"And Mickie's your...?"

"Cousin."

"Hey, how many cousins do you have?"

"Seven. Mickie, Claire, Katie, Rose, Nathan, Ryan and TJ. How many cousins do you have?"

"One. Her name's Gigi. I'm an only child, and I only have one cousin. Big family, huh?" I caught his obvious sarcasm.

"Emily has two older sisters and fifteen cousins. Plus, she's already an aunt."

"Emily's your friend who isn't here?" he asked to make sure. "Hey, do you have siblings?"

"Yes."

"To which one?"

"Both. My brother's name is Luke." I wondered about how interesting this conversation was… If I was Ben I don't think I'd find it interesting. "Anyway, why'd you call?" I asked. "I know it wasn't to learn about my family."

"Oh. I wanted to ask you if you wanted to go horseback riding on Wednesday. That is your day off, isn't it?"

"Yeah, I have Wednesday off. Sure, I'd love to go."

"You'll probably want to wear jeans. And don't eat lunch, we're having a picnic."

"When and where am I meeting you?"

"Where the taxi picked us up after our first date, at…"

"How about noon?" I asked. I definitely wanted to sleep more than I normally did.

"Yeah, that's fine," Ben agreed.

"So, are you coming to see me at work tomorrow and Tuesday?" I questioned.

"Probably," he said, acting like he had something better to do. I whined. If he were here, I would have punched him. Not hard, though. "Fine. Yeah, I'll come. You're going to cost me a fortune!"

"Well, I'll be worth it."

"Yeah, I think so too."

"I have to go now…" I replied, sad now.

"Okay. Bye. See you tomorrow," he said.

"Yup," I agreed.

June 16th

Pink Bedroom

Ha! Ben made fun of Mr. Poe today. Creepy went up to Ben because he's been at work with me for long periods of time without eating a lot. Ben just made this comment that made Creepy blush. But Creepy insisted anyway.

"I thought the customer was always right," Ben had replied.

"You're not a customer," Creep said.

"Oh, really?" Ben asked, gesturing to his Coke and plate of buffalo wings.

"Fine." And then Creepy stomped off! Seriously, he STOMPED!

Besides that, my day has been really similar to every other day. I can't wait until Wednesday!

"Good morning, Maddi," Holly greeted me. "What are you doing with Ben tomorrow?"

"Didn't I tell you yesterday?"

"Yeah, but I forgot."

"Tell you on the way to work," I said, noticing Aunt Annie coming towards us.

"Okay."

"Morning, girls," Aunt Annie said when she came into the kitchen. "We only have a little time left to figure out the puzzle. Do you want to help?"

"Sure. We have half an hour," I replied, getting up to wash my bowl.

Holly and I walked into the family room, and sat on the floor around the old, round, wood table with most of a puzzle put together on it. The hard wood floor was somehow way more comfortable than the faded blue couch with its breaking frame and paper thin cushions. We started sifting through the pieces in the boxes, and identified and fit ten pieces in several minutes.

"Oh my gosh!" Holly yelled when her phone alarm went off. "We have to leave now, or we'll be late for work!"

"Okay. Bye, Aunt Annie," I yelled as we ran out the door, jumped on our bikes, and raced towards the Gate House.

"Okay, so what are you doing tomorrow?" Holly asked as we left our driveway.

"Ben and I are horseback – whoa!" I exclaimed as we started down the hill. The sudden speed and wind blowing in my face surprised me. I almost flew off my bike. At the bottom, I tried again. "Horseback riding on trails, and eating a picnic lunch."

"Fun!"

"Yeah," I said, when we walked in the door of the Gate House. It was quiet for a couple seconds.

"Hey, isn't your birthday tomorrow?" Holly asked.

"Yup."

"Does Ben know that?"

"Nope."

"Oh. Just making sure – you're turning seventeen, right?" Holly and I locked our bikes where a bunch of racks were.

"Yes, Holly. I'm not turning eighteen yet. You're older than me, and have been your whole life!"

"Hey, just checking. My memory's not as good as yours."

"You're calling my awful memory good?"

"Yeah. When's my birthday?"

"June tenth. Only eight days before mine," I answered automatically.

"When's Emily's?"

"November first."

"What's the first thing Ben said to you?"

"Are you okay?" I answered, with nearly no hesitation.

"Yeah…" Holly said, a strange look of confusion crossing her face.

"No, I meant that as what Ben first said to me." Who could forget? I tripped over stuffed animals while I was staring at him!

"Why did he say that?"

"Because I tripped and fell."

"Oh! You've got to tell me that story."

"Okay, but Creepy looks mad," I said. Mr. Poe was walking toward us, glaring. The whole time we had been talking, we were standing at the hostess stand. There weren't any people coming in to eat in my section, so what was the deal?

"Ladies! Only one person should be at the hostess stand. Okay?"

"Yes." We smiled, knowing we were going to laugh. We burst when he was out of earshot. I laughed so hard I fell down, but I stayed there, sliding back so my back was against the hostess stand.

"Stop laughing! I can't laugh when I'm showing people to their table!" Holly pleaded. I stopped and put on a straight face, but that made Holly giggle.

"Shh!" I whispered. So Holly showed the couple to a table that wasn't in my section. Mine was empty, but Sara, the strawberry blonde girl who tried to steal Ben, had a full section. And it wasn't because I did a bad job. But then I realized something when Holly came back. "Holly, I actually need money – seat people in my section – tips please!"

"Really? Okay. Here's one. Kiss me, crazy person, and I'll consider not leaving," a voice that was not Holly's said.

"Hi, Ben!" I exclaimed, wobbly standing up so I could hug him. "I would, but considering what the Creep's already done today, I think he's watching us."

"Okay," Ben said. Holly shooed me away from Ben by saying somebody wanted my attention. I left my friends, but was puzzled when I looked around and saw no one seated in my section. I glanced at Holly, who was obviously up to something, as she slowly walked with Ben to his usual table.

"I know you aren't our waitress, but we really need drink refills," a man was saying.

"What did you have?"

"We both had Diet Coke."

"I'll go get those for you." I grabbed their empty cups and headed back to the machine. Several seconds later I came back with their new drinks and set them down. Exciting! I found Ben and walked over to him. "Do you want anything besides Coke today?" I asked.

"Yeah, but I have a feeling you won't let me have it," he replied.

I was pretty sure I knew what was coming next, but I still said, "What?"

"Come to dinner with me tonight."

"I can't. Family stuff. It *is* a family vacation." There it was. The excuse I always had to make sure Aunt Annie didn't know.

"Fine." Ben pouted like a little kid.

"I'm hanging out with you tomorrow!"

"Yeah, but that's not enough."

"Oh well. I'll go get your Coke. I need to serve my other customers. See you in a bit." I turned around.

"Maddi, wait!" Ben called. I faced him again. He grabbed the collar of my shirt, pulled me down to his eye level, and kissed me. Then he let me leave. I walked away feeling a little guilty and with my heart racing. I made my usual speech introducing myself, wrote down and fetched orders, and talked with Ben a little for the next hour and a half. Ben left around 1:00. Clearing his table, I noticed a note on some paper.

> Maddi – I obviously paid the gratuity that's on the bill. But I hang out here to see you, and I take you places when I can. Do I not spend enough on you? Just kidding. Call you later!
> – Ben

Just his promise of calling me made the hours of work fly by. Before I knew it, Holly was calling my name, telling me it was time to go.

Devon Warriner   ----------   Get Over it

Devon Warriner   ----------   Get Over it

June 17th

Pink Bedroom

I love Ben! I know I do. Mrs. Madison Campo. Okay, I'm getting ahead of myself. I'm only (almost) seventeen, and we've known each other about a week. But what's wrong with fantasizing? That'd be amazing!

Okay, I shouldn't do that. It'll make me act freaky around him.

My phone rang, playing a really old song. It was from the '80's, and it was *Take My Breath Away* by Berlin. I'd programmed it as Ben's ring. Although the title was true, I hadn't picked it because of the title. It was a good song, and it *did* fit the person nicely.

"Hey, Ben!"

"Hi, Maddi. Did you get my note?"

"Yeah. Like you can't afford to pay a tip on Coke and maybe something else when you actually eat something!"

"What if I can't?"

"I find that highly unlikely."

"But what if it's true?" Ben asked again. My attitude changed completely.

"Is it?" I whisper-asked. I didn't care if he was poor, but he didn't seem like it.

"No. I was just kidding."

"Oh my gosh! Don't do that!"

"Why? Did I freak you out? Would you break up with me if I was poor?" he joked.

"No. But... never mind." I decided against saying what I thought.

"Good. So we're on for tomorrow?"

"Yeah. We're going horseback riding and having a picnic, right?" I questioned.

"Yup. Picnic in front of the fort. Then we're walking to Jack's stable, which is around the corner from Turtle Toys and the Gate House. We're going on a trail I know. It should be fun."

"Sounds it." I yawned, and I could feel my eyelids drooping. "Ben, I'm really tired, do you mind if I go now so I can sleep?"

"Nope. Goodnight!" Ben replied.

"Night." I shut my phone and slid into my bed, under the covers. Reaching over, I turned out the lamp so I could get to sleep and Holly could really sleep. I soon drifted into oblivion.

* * *

My phone started playing *Safety Dance* by Men Without Hats at 8:00 AM. It had nothing to do with the person calling, either. I just liked the song. I rolled over, wondering who would call me on my birthday at 8:00 AM. I managed to open one eye, grabbed my phone and glanced at the screen. Gabi. Gabi had short brown hair and dark chocolate-colored eyes. She had glasses with black frames that look really good on her, but she usually wore contacts. And for some reason, she was up at 8:00 calling me. Gabi is *not* a morning person, so I was wary. I sat up in bed and flipped open my phone.

"What song did your phone just play?" she asked.

"Well, hello to you, too!" I said.

"Hi. What song?" she persisted.

"*Safety Dance.*"

"I'm telling you, make it play a Jonas Brothers song!" she exclaimed.

"Why?" I asked. Gabi gasped.

"Why?! Because they're amazing!"

"I don't think so," I replied. I heard her gasp again, and she hung up. I just waited. There had to be a reason for her to call me. Two seconds later, my phone lit up and started playing *Safety Dance* again.

"Hi. What now?" I answered.

"I just wanted to tell you happy birthday before I forgot," she replied.

"At eight o'clock in the morning? Why are you up this early?" I questioned.

"I've got a busy day today."

"Me too. Speaking of which, I have to get ready for the day. Thanks for the birthday call!"

"Okay. Bye!" Gabi replied. I quickly hung up my phone as I still had to eat, take a shower, brush my teeth, pick my clothes, and put on makeup, all in time to meet Ben at noon. And I had to walk down there. I got out of bed and went downstairs to eat, not bothering to change because I was in sweatpants and a t-shirt. 8:00 AM. Ugh. Mickie was already up, and so was Holly. Mickie had probably been up for at least an hour already, but she was just now eating. Holly was eating too. I grabbed a bowl, spoon, and some Frosted Flakes from the kitchen. Holly had milk on the table. Then I walked in the breakfast room and sat on the bench that didn't have an ugly green cushion. Holly was across from me, and Mickie was next to me.

"Morning, you guys," I greeted as I poured my breakfast into my bowl.

"Why are you up so early?" Holly asked. I tried to answer, but Mickie was singing 'Happy Birthday'.

"Thanks, Mickie," I said when she finished. "Gabi called and woke me up."

"Seriously? Doesn't she usually sleep in?"

"Apparently not today," I replied.

"What are you doing on your birthday?" Mickie asked, trying to get into the conversation.

"Hanging out with Holly." All of a sudden, I felt guilty. I wasn't hanging out with Holly. I was ditching her.

"Why don't you hang out with me?"

"Because we're going all over today."

"No, I mean at all!"

"I work most days, Mickie. And I like to go places on my days off. I'd love to hang out with you."

"I can go places."

"Not without your parents."

"If I went with you…"

"Sorry, Mick, I can't." I didn't want to hurt her feelings, but I sort of had to. She left the room pouting.

"She could go downtown with us sometime," Holly suggested.

"Yeah, but not when I have a date. Which reminds me. Are you sure that you're okay with me hanging out with Ben."

"Yeah. I'll probably go shopping. Maybe I'll meet a guy." Holly smiled. "Or, maybe not. When you and Ben get back, though, come hang with me."

"Okay. I'll call you. And shh!" I finished my cereal, and went upstairs to take a shower. With only one shower in the house, I was lucky to find it empty. I took my shower, letting the hot water calm me down, but still hurrying in case the warm water ran out. I was done in ten minutes, and I got dressed in my sweatpants and shirt again so I could run downstairs and tell everyone I was blow-drying my hair. We'd blown the fuse several times by using too many things at once. By 8:45, I was getting dressed for real. I guessed I could have slept more. Grabbing my jeans – the only pair I'd brought – I put them on and looked through my shirts. I finally decided on a white t-shirt with a light blue tank top over it. The tank had spaghetti straps, and had a green band right under my boobs and at the bottom of the tank. I pulled out my makeup bag. I knew I was using eyeliner, mascara, and the pale pink gloss, but could I put eye shadow on? Every day I put on those products, but I never put on eye shadow in the summer. So I decided just to put on what I had already pulled out of the bag. When I finished, it was only 9:00. Ugh. Gabi's fault. I called her and whispered "seven days..." when I got her voicemail. It was one of our inside jokes we stole from another group and made even funnier. In a louder voice, I said, "You'll pay. Wait and see."

"You have three hours, you know," I heard Holly say. She was in the doorway, leaning against the frame.

"I know. I'm calling him and asking to meet at eleven instead."

"But you still have two hours."

"Yeah, I know. What do you want to do?"

"No idea. Let's go use your uncle's computer."

"Okay. But let me call Ben first." Holly sat on her bed as I called Ben. "Hey, Ben. Can we meet at eleven instead of noon?"

"Sure!" Ben said enthusiastically. For some reason, I think he liked that time better.

"Great. See you then!" I said. We both hung up. "Okay, Holly. Let's go do whatever!"

"Hey, do you mind if I check my email?" Holly asked me after we got permission to use the computer.

"Nope. As long as I can check mine too." So Holly got on her email, and had twelve unread messages. Twelve! Of course, seven of them were from Barnes and Noble, Aeropostle, or American Eagle. But two of them were from Sami, another was from Gabi, and the last two were from Emily. I wondered if I had that many. After she was done, I got on my email, and I had fourteen unread messages. I had the same store emails Holly did, and the same number of emails from people, but I also had two from my other friend, Luisa.

"Now what?" Holly asked after I logged off.

"Um… I don't know. This was your idea."

"Go to that one website with all those random games. You know, the one with the drawing game and a version of Deal or No Deal?" So we played all the games on that site that looked fun. "Hey, Maddi, it's ten-thirty. Do you want to leave yet?"

"Yeah. We're walking, so let's go now."

"Okay. Bye, Mickie!" Holly called to my cousin.

"Bye!" I heard her reply. Holly and I walked the way we always took on our bikes, down the hill, past the restaurant, and onto Market Street. Although Holly was going to turn off on Astor Street to get to the main street, she realized she had to get a map at the tourism center, the building across the street from the fort. I stopped by the wood bike racks, half-way down the hill that was Fort Street. She understood why and kept going.

"Bye, Maddi! See you later!"

"Yeah, bye!" I said. She jogged down the rest of the hill and disappeared into the building. I walked slowly past the Gazebo shaped Mackinac Tours ticket booth. "Hey, Ben!" I exclaimed when I saw him by the building. I ran up to him, and he leaned down to kiss me. My phone started ringing, playing *Crazy Frog*. "Sorry, Ben, do you mind if I answer this?" I asked, pulling away from the kiss.

'Yes," he said firmly, pulling me back and kissing me again. For a second I didn't want to answer my phone either, but it rang again and broke the moment.

"Too bad," I teased. I pulled back again and flipped open my phone. "Hey, Em!"

"Happy birthday!" she shouted. I winced.

"Do you have to yell in my ear?" I asked.

"Yup."

"Emily!" I exclaimed.

"I know you hate it when people call and sing to you on the phone, but you're going to have to endure it today!" Emily then proceeded to sing 'Happy Birthday' to me, sounding terrible on the phone.

"Thanks," I said when she finished. Ben was motioning to me to hang up.

"...today?" I heard Emily ask.

"I'm sorry, what?"

"Oh, I know what that means. Are you with your boyfriend?"

"Yes," I replied, giggling because Ben was trying to kiss me again.

"Okay. Call me later!"

"I will!"

"Love ya!" Emily said.

"You too. Bye!"

"Bye." I hung up after that. Ben looked happy. Kind of like a puppy happy to see his master. Funny, really.

"Happy birthday!" he said. "Why didn't you tell me it was your birthday today?"

"I don't know... It's not a big deal."

"Well, let's go," he suggested, picking up a picnic basket. Oh. My. Gosh. I thought he would just bring a bag! We sat on the grass, and he pulled two sandwiches, some chips, and lemonade out of the old school basket. It was a cliché picnic. The sandwiches were peanut butter and jelly, and the chips were tortilla. That was good. Potato chips taste bad.

"Mmm…" I said, with some exaggeration. A lie, yes.

"Oh, come on liar! You don't have to fake, it's just sandwiches and chips."

"Okay." We ate the food quickly.

"Do you want dessert?" he asked.

"What dessert?"

"This," he said, pulling a cake out of the basket. It said "Happy Birthday Maddi!" on it. This wasn't a cliché picnic dessert. That would have been Jell-o or something.

"Yeah. But how'd you know?"

"Holly told me once when I came to the Gate House."

"Blabbermouth," I said. Ben laughed.

"How come you hate people calling and singing 'Happy Birthday'?" Ben asked.

"Because it sounds *horrible* on the phone! Even if they're awesome singers, like Emily."

"Emily's an awesome singer?"

"Yeah. She was in the Follies, a talent show, in our town a few times, singing a solo!"

"That's cool."

"Yeah, she and my other friends are amazing!"

"I think you're more amazing," Ben said.

"Aw. Aren't you sweet?" I said. My stomach had turned again when he said that, and I felt so happy. "But I'll have some of that cake now," I exclaimed happily. Ben handed me a fork.

"Dig in." I looked at him questioningly. "I didn't bring plates." He grabbed a fork, too, after he said this, and took a bite. I did too. It was lemon cake with vanilla frosting. My favorite.

"Did Holly tell you what cake I liked too?" I asked.

"No." Ben looked confused.

"This is my favorite kind of cake."

"Huh! Well, this is *my* favorite flavor cake, and I thought you might like it too."

"Well, I do." We finished what we could of the cake pretty quickly. "Are we walking down to the stable?" I asked, standing up.

"Yup. Ready to go?" Ben stood up too.

"Yeah, of course. Let's go." Ben grabbed my hand, and we started walking up the Fort Street hill, to Market Street. We had to walk all the way to Cadotte Avenue, the street that was the Grand Hotel Hill, but we turned down Mahoney Avenue, a road that started just before we would have reached Great Turtle Toys and my place of work. Usually I just whizzed past these streets to get where I was going on my bike. But walking slowly, hand in hand with Ben, I noticed all the pretty scenery and even the street names, too.

"Hello, kids!" A man greeted us when we got to the stable.

"Hey, Andy. We need two horses. Oh, and can you keep this basket while we ride?"

"Done and done," Andy replied. "Are you a beginner?" he asked me.

"Well, I think I'm a natural at horse riding, but yeah, I've only done it a few times."

"Okay, then you should take Ash," he said, showing me a dappled gray horse. Then he turned to Ben. "Do you want Twilight?" he asked.

"Yes, please." Andy then brought out a black horse with a white diamond on his face. Soon after that, we set out, just the two of us. It hurt a little. It was really bouncy when the horses trotted.

"You ride often?" I asked. Talking was hard, my voice bounced along with my body. "You know Andy."

"Yeah, I ride weekly." I waited, but when he didn't elaborate, I asked a new question.

"Are these mares or colts?"

"Twilight is a male horse. Ash is a mare, Twilight's her dad."

"What, you don't know what a male horse is called?" Ben smiled as I asked this.

"I do. But you don't."

"I thought male horses weren't actually called stallions. If I'm wrong, then teach me, oh wise one!" I laughed.

"Male horses are geldings if they're fixed. And colts are male foals, or babies. But Twilight is a stallion, he isn't fixed. You got the mare part right."

"Oh really?"

"Yeah." By now we were on a trail, with no one else in sight.

"Okay," I said, feeling awkward.

"Be quiet and look around you!" Ben exclaimed.

"Why? I'd rather talk to you," I whined, sounding like a petulant four-year-old. Or Mickie, actually.

"Shut up. Please."

"Fine. Sheesh!" I remained silent for a few minutes. I could hear animals in the trees. But I was impatient. "Can we talk now?"

"Yeah, I guess. I'm always quiet in the area because it reminds me of my mom when she rode horses. She loved woods like these." Ben didn't sound sad, so I didn't think his mom died, but he wasn't happy either. I glanced around him since he was leading, and was happy when I saw the path widening. I rode up next to him.

"What?" he asked. I wordlessly leaned over and kissed him, managing to not fall out of my saddle. Somehow, we halted our horses at the same time. It was only after some time had elapsed that we pulled apart. I stared at him, wondering how it was that I could be falling in love with him after knowing him for so little time. Maybe it was a feeling of a love struck teenager, but I thought it was true. Then I got caught up in the sea of his blue eyes and could not pull myself out. If they actually were a sea, and I in them, I would have drowned. "Well, that was dangerous. What do you say we return the horses," Ben started.

"No!" I said, thinking our date would be over then, forgetting about Holly waiting for me.

"I wasn't finished, goofball. We return the horses and find a bench...?" Ben suggested.

"A day full of clichés. But there are no benches anywhere. Except the school playground," I replied, trying to remember any other places that had benches.

"Ha! I was only joking about the bench. But we could go hang out somewhere with one."

"Okay. Let's go fly a kite, up to the highest height," I started to sing.

"Well, no, but..."

"Hey, I was just singing," I interrupted.

"I know."

"Where are we going?"

"Have you been to the library?" Ben asked.

"With all its books? Of course, I *am* an insatiable reader. But the layout is confusing."

"Need a tour?" he questioned.

"No. I always bring my own books."

"Oh. Well, we can go to British Landing, or either of the bluffs, or Sugar Loaf," Ben suggested. Sugar Loaf was an interesting shaped rock my family liked to climb around and explore.

"How about the bluff that's just past the Grand?" I asked. "Hey! There's a bench there!" Ben smiled as I said this.

"Yeah, but that wasn't the reason. It's so beautiful."

"Which bluff is that one?"

"The west," he answered.

"Where's East Bluff?"

"Almost by Mission Point."

"Oh," I said.

"Ready to go?"

"Of course." Soon we got back to the stable. Andy took our horses and Ben grabbed the basket. We walked up the hills, and took the turn that would take us in front of the Grand Hotel.

"It looks even better at sunset," Ben said when we had almost reached the bluff.

"Yeah, I know."

"Oh." We sat down on the huge bench with its chipping paint that was miraculously free of sand and gravel. The cement bench was cold, so we cuddled together and stared at the sky and the Mackinac bridge for several minutes. I turned to look at him, putting my back against the wide side of the bench and pulling my legs up in front of me. He turned to look at me at the same time. He leaned in to kiss me, and when we pulled apart, we still sat staring at each other. My heart was racing, but not very loudly, thank goodness.

"Oh my gosh, I have to go!" I exclaimed after I had glanced at my watch nervously. Ben jumped but quickly recovered.

"Okay. I think I forgot to say this earlier, but you're more beautiful than the view here." My eyes teared up and I turned away. He had said something like this earlier too. Such lines. Even if they *were* lines, they were still amazing to hear. The sound of his voice was so captivating. Ben made me face him. "I'll call you later."

I found my voice a second later. "Thanks. And yeah," I replied lamely. I couldn't even think of any really popular lines to say back to him. While I was trying to come up with something, Ben kissed me again. His arms around me filled me with warmth, but also gave me goosebumps.

"Bye, Maddi," he whispered as he turned me around and shoved me toward the Grand Hotel. Somehow he knew I wasn't going home yet.

"Bye, Ben," I called back at him. He hadn't moved yet. He smiled and waved.

Still dazed, like I had been after our first kiss, I made my way downtown. I realized I was there when I reached the road I normally turned at. I pulled out my phone.

"Hey, Holly. Where are you?" I asked.

"Um… the park."

"Where?" I didn't understand.

"Marquette Park. You call it the fort yard."

"Oh."

"Why, is your date with Ben over?" Holly asked.

"Yup."

"Then come hang out. I'm just working on some new designs."

"Okay. Can't wait to see them. I'll be there in a few minutes," I said.

"Bye, Maddi."

"Bye." I shut my phone and shoved it in my pocket.

All of a sudden, frustrated that I hadn't ridden my bike downtown, I sprinted to the fort. Thankfully, it was only a few blocks down the street I was already on.

"Hey! That was quick." Holly glanced up at me when my shadow fell over her.

"Yeah, well, I was downtown," I replied. "What are you designing today?"

"Clothes you should wear. Maybe on your next date," Holly said. Her tone seemed a little bitter, and she hadn't shown me her drawings yet.

"Sorry I've been ditching you. I haven't meant to, and I won't do it anymore," I apologized.

"It's okay. You think you're in love," she replied.

"How do you know I'm not actually in love?"

"I didn't say you weren't." Not knowing how to answer, I shut up for a second.

"Can I see?"

"Yeah, I guess," Holly replied, handing me her sketchbook. She leaned over to show me as I finally plopped down beside her. "I don't have colors with me, so you can't tell what they'll really look like. At least, not yet anyway."

"That's fine. Tell me about the colors."

"Okay, so the skirt here is white," Holly said, pointing to a skirt that was cut at an angle so one leg was more bare than the other. "I haven't figured out the top color yet, but it starts darker at the bottom and gets lighter at the top. I was thinking blue or purple or some other color like that. And on this one," Holly continued, pointing to another outfit that had a mini-skirt with a triangle cut out on the bottom and two tank tops or camisoles layered together. "The skirt would be like jeans. You know, that darker denim blue? I was thinking the tank top should be a darker pink, and the cami under it should be white." The tank top had sequin-type things above the band that would run right above my stomach if I was wearing it. The cami she drew under it had lace at the top that would make the tanks look pretty together. "And the heart necklace I drew there would either be red with a silver chain, or silver with pink crystals covering it, also with a silver chain."

I spaced a little while she continued her explanations. She was so into them. But I came back when she started talking about one of the two dresses she had drawn.

"Obviously you shouldn't wear this. At least not here. Maybe to a dance." Holly was pointing at the dress that had tiny bubbles drawn on it going in spirals and other patterns. The dress was cut the same way most of the shirts were, with a band under my boobs. My favorite cut on dresses. "All these little bubbles below the band are these silver things. They remind me of a cross between rhinestones and sequins, but they're better. This dress would be really light blue, especially at that part. Above the band it's cut in this way that I can't describe. But all those little lines actually would look like folds in the fabric, and it'd be a darker blue than below. I think the straps should be either silver, blue, or maybe even white. It's not strapless because I know you don't like strapless dresses. The necklace is really simple. The pendant looks like a pearl drop on a silver chain." Holly kept describing this dress. This one was so obviously her favorite of all her designs today.

"Holly, I love that dress. All of these designs are amazing. I think that should be your job when you get one. Just be a designer," I said.

"I don't know. I'm not sure I could do it. I like designing for myself and my friends, because I know your styles, and it's fun."

"Other people have the same styles we do. If you just designed things we would like, you would be guaranteed at least one customer, because *we* would buy it. And other people would too. You could guess that."

"Yeah... Maybe."

"Not maybe. I think you should do it."

"Okay. More than maybe, but not yes. I've got more options," Holly decided.

"That's good."

We kept talking about possibilities in the future... just for our jobs. We talked more about clothes, and we talked about college. Everything was not that far away. When we went back to school, we would be seniors, and then when we graduated, we would go to college. And four or five years later, we would definitely *have* to get jobs if we didn't already have them. It was hard to talk about.

"Holly, are you thirsty too?" I asked, feeling my throat with all its dryness.

"Yeah. But I don't have any more money with me."

"Did you buy something?"

"Yeah, pencils and paper."

"Oh. Okay. Time to go home. No money, right?"

"Right."

"Neither do I. Come on, let's walk."

Holly and I wearily trudged back to Dufina, the cottage with the funny name. Okay, I knew it was someone's last name, and lots of people had funny last names. But Dufina was just really funny to me.

"Maddi, breathe. I think you're high."

"Seriously?" I asked. I realized I had been giggling.

"No, I don't seriously think you're high. If you were high off anything, it would be the nitrogen in the air. And that doesn't affect anyone. So that answer is no. I don't think you're high."

"Oh. Okay."

Holly told me about her day on the way home. She discovered the lookout on Fort Holmes, Skull Cave, and the Ste. Anne's Cemetery. She had found the Dufina name on some headstones. Then she walked the trails from Arch Rock toward the East Bluff, nearly falling down a steep cliff. She made it back downtown and relaxed in the park, where I had found her designing clothes.

June 18th

Pink Bedroom

Okay. That was definitely one of the best birthdays ever. Very possibly *the* best.

Ben surprised me with a cake! It was lemon, and amazing. I wonder if he made it... or if someone else did. I should ask. And then the rest of the date with him was amazing too! I mean, horseback riding? I guess we didn't ride that long. But it was fun. And then, continuing our day of clichés, we sat on a bench. And "made out" a little. But not seriously.

And I got Holly to make up with me. I don't know when she started to be mad at me, but she's not really anymore. And just hanging out today was great. It's like we usually do.

And then I got to choose what we had for dinner. I asked for meatballs, so of course we had spaghetti and meatballs. Normally I would have asked for something so much better, but I love the meatballs. I think we already had spaghetti and meatballs once during this trip... I don't remember though. I guess I'm not paying much attention to dinners.

Aunt Annie made white cake. I'm making her chocolate cake for her birthday, which is on the 23rd. So... yeah. It was awesome. Mickie helped decorate it; there were all these squiggles made of that gel stuff that can be used to decorate cakes and cookies.

    And then I opened presents from my family. I mostly got books. Mickie got me the next book in one of my favorite series. It's one of the *many* series about vampires. I had read the first one, and the next had come out in April. But... not having much money and not being able to convince Mom to buy it, I didn't get it until now. Aunt Annie and Uncle Chuck, having given me all the seasons of *Gilmore Girls* on DVD already, and obviously not being able to think of anything else, also bought me a book. This one is about dragons, and it is the third in the series. It actually came out in hardcover in 2007, but again, money. Mom and Dad said my gifts were at home, I'll open them later. And Holly said my gift was at home, she had forgotten it. So I'll have another birthday when we get home.

    This birthday was great. Now I'm starting that vampire book!

My phone went off early for the second day in a row. But this time, I meant for it to. Sort of. I had set the alarm, but I guess I messed up the time. 7:00 AM was too early! I fixed the alarm, laid back down and tried to go to sleep again.

"So, Maddi, you never actually told me about your date yesterday," Holly said. I turned over to look at her. She was laying on her pillow staring at me. So much for sleeping more. Oh well.

"Okay, fine Holly. You win. I won't go back to sleep, I'll tell you." I was just teasing, but Holly didn't realize it.

"Hey! I thought you were up."

"Oh, forget it, Holls. He made me a cake. Thanks, by the way," I murmured sarcastically.

"He did? Oh my gosh, I didn't tell him to do *that*! I mean..." Holly stopped, realizing she had just told me that she had told Ben it was my birthday.

"I knew you told him Holls. He snitched on you."

"Oh. Go on."

"Yup. It was cliché-full. The picnic, besides the cake, was typical picnic food. He brought a basket. An actual picnic basket, which I didn't think he would do. We rode horses for maybe thirty minutes."

"Why so short?"

"'Cause... we wanted to do other things," I hinted.

"Dirty!" Holly exclaimed.

"Just kidding! And that's unlike you. But we did go to West Bluff, the one near the cottage, and sat on a bench and..."

"Another cliché?"

"Yup. But then I jumped up and said I had to go, because I realized the time and thought that I shouldn't ditch you so long," I finished. Holly made a face when I said 'ditch'.

"Oh thanks," Holly said sarcastically.

"And... that's it." I concluded, because I knew Holly was waiting for more.

"There isn't any more?"

"Nope. Deal with it."

"Fine."

"I'm hungry. I'm getting breakfast now," I told Holly. I got up really quickly and left the bedroom. I knew she would press for more. She wouldn't believe that I *was* telling her everything. I wasn't hiding anything, but I just didn't feel like going through it. I know that it's normal to go over every detail a thousand times with friends, but for some reason, I just didn't feel like sharing.

"Hey, Maddi!" Mickie greeted me when I got downstairs.

"Good morning, Mick."

"Do you have to work today again?" she somewhat whined.

"Yeah. I'm sorry, Mickie. I wasn't thinking about how much I couldn't hang out with you when I took the job."

"Okay. Fine. Can you stay with me next time you have the day off?" Mickie requested.

"Maybe. It depends on what Holly wants."

"But you hang out with her every day off, and every other day!" she complained.

"Fine. I will hang out with you. But maybe not the whole day, okay?"

"Yeah. Fine," she interjected. I realized then that Holly had been standing behind me almost the whole time.

"Fine by me. Just not the whole day, Mickie. The morning," Holly said.

"Okay." Holly and I went in the next room.

"Thanks, Holly."

"For what? My cousins always want to hang out with me too. And I want to play with them. I know what you both are feeling, and I know you're busy. Your boyfriend keeps you busy when you have time when we're not working!"

"Are you jealous?" I asked. "I apologized yesterday, and I'm not ditching you anymore."

Holly stood there for a second, not moving. "Yeah, I think I am jealous," she admitted.

"Okay. I'm still sorry, Holls. I will hang out with you and Mickie too, not just Ben."

"I know. But I can't shake the jealousy. I guess once the monster attaches, he never wants to detach."

"What makes you think the big green jealousy monster is a guy?" I asked. Holly laughed.

"I wouldn't know, and neither would you. Neither of us have ever met the monster."

"Maybe I have. I mean, I met the bogey-man," I suggested.

"Sure you did," Holly replied sarcastically. "And I met Dracula."

"Okay, maybe I didn't. But I made you laugh!"

"Yeah... Meeting a vampire sounds good. Even the weird normal ones that will drink my blood."

"Ugh. Are you referring to *Twilight*?"

"Yup. Don't you like the books?"

"Yeah. I read them first, remember? But I don't want to meet Dracula, I'd rather meet Edward!"

"But if you can get Dracula to stop sucking your blood, you can be a vampire and meet all the others," Holly said.

"I don't think it's true with Dracula. I think it only works with the vampires in *Twilight*. Plus, you know they aren't real, right?"

"I refuse to believe that."

"Are you going to start calling yourself Alice again?"

"I never stopped. Come here, please," Holly replied. So I followed her upstairs and into the bedroom. She opened her notebook where she had some of the assignments she had to do over the summer. Where her name should have been, she had written "Alice".

"You know the teachers won't know who Alice is? And they'll say you didn't turn anything in."

"Yeah, I know. I'll change them right before I turn them in."

"You could just write 'Holly', you know," I said.

"Yeah, but that's no fun."
"Whatever."

"Miss? Can I order now?"

"Of course," I replied, tiring fast. I had only been at work for an hour and a half. I wrote down his order and left to tell the cooks.

"Maddi?" I jumped at my name, since even though I told the customers, they didn't call me by my name, and I didn't hear it much. I realized it was another waitress who said it. She was older than me, but only in her later twenties, and her name was Laura. I didn't think she knew my name. After all, most people didn't absorb names like I did. If I heard it, I knew it. Maybe she was the same way.

"Yeah?"

"Are you okay? You seem tired, but mostly anxious. Somehow at the same time."

"Yeah, I'm fine," I started. I wondered if I should be telling her this, but I disregarded the thought. "Yesterday was my birthday, and I had a great date with my boyfriend. But I'm hiding it from my family, and my four-year-old cousin wants my attention more, and so does Holly," I said, gesturing toward where Holly stood.

"Why are you hiding it?"

"Gossip-y aunt."

"Oh. I was thinking of something else."

"Yeah, I know. Romeo and Juliet type thoughts? You know, parents who don't like the boy?"

"Yeah, actually. I think you should tell them. Your mom and dad first," she hesitated here, probably wondering if I had both or if they were here. "Then your aunt and cousin. Tell your aunt while you two are alone and ask her not to broadcast it or gossip about it."

"Thanks, that's really good advice," I replied, knowing I would never do that. It sounded too perfect. But I put on my smile as I thanked her and left.

"You're welcome," she called after me.

"Ben's here," Holly told me as I passed her.

"No, dip, Sherlock."

"Hey, I didn't know if you knew yet."

"I did and I was kidding."

"Oh. Go talk to him."

"Fine." I left Holly and walked over to Ben. I was immediately in a better mood, because I always felt so happy when I was around him.

"Hey," he said.

"Hi," I replied, wishing I could kiss him.

"So when you left yesterday, was it for Holly?" he asked.

"Yeah."

"Well, tell me that next time. I understand loyalty to friends, and I was monopolizing your time."

"Seriously?"

"Yes, seriously. I understand. I really..." I waited as he paused, wondering if this would be it, "care about you, and if you need time with your friend on vacation, I won't care. After all, you brought her here, and it seems mean to abandon her."

"Okay. I will next time. Next time we go out, can we do something Holly can too? I felt really bad earlier when she was mad at me. She said I *was* abandoning her."

"Sure. Speaking of which, can we do something Friday or Saturday?"

"No. Dinner on Friday, as always, with my family, and church on Saturday evening right after work."

"Can I come to church with you?"

"You're not Catholic!"

"Does that mean I can't come in to church with you?"

"No, I guess not. But you can't receive communion."

"That's fine."

"But we can't really *do* anything but church on Saturday since I have to get home."

"Okay. What about Sunday?"

"What about it?"

"You work then too, don't you?"

"Yeah."

"And you can't miss dinner once?"

"Well... maybe I can. Depends on what it is, and if Holly's coming."

"I was thinking a movie. Yes, Holly can come to a movie."

"Then possibly, yes."

"Okay. Talk to Holly, and call me later." Ben got up to leave.

"You're not staying for anything?"

"No, but I'll be here tomorrow."

"Okay. Talk to you later," I said as he started walking.

"Yup." Ben squeezed my hand before he let go. Funny, I hadn't noticed him grabbing my hand. I walked over to where Holly was.

"Well, what'd he want?"

"He wants to come with me to church Saturday after work, and to a movie Sunday. You're coming too. But we need to tell my family something."

"More lying. Great, Maddi. Just tell them!"

"I can't. You know I can't. So do you want to come Sunday?"

"Sure. But where on the island is there a place to see movies?"

"I didn't think anywhere, but Ben must know somewhere. I'll ask him tonight when I call him."

"Okay."

"Hi. You've reached Ben's phone. I'm obviously not able to answer right now, but I'll call you back if you leave a message." That was Ben's voicemail.

"Hey, Ben. I was just calling about our plans. Call me back, okay?" Then I waited a few seconds, feeling dumb. He couldn't answer, obviously. He even said it. "Bye!"

"So what's his voicemail?" Holly asked. She was sitting in the bedroom with me when I called him.

"Oh, the normal one most everyone uses. Obviously some important person calls him sometime."

"Oh, yeah. Obviously," she said sarcastically.

"I just meant that maybe his boss calls him or something."

"Okay, I'll stop teasing."

"Good. It doesn't seem like either of us are too good at taking it."

"And are you saying your voicemail isn't normal?"

"Yeah. It's not. Making fun of commercials and playing kids' songs are not normal."

"Well, a lot of people use songs."

"But do they use songs the Cookie Monster sings?"

"No, I guess not."

"Crazy people have crazy voicemail messages."

"Yeah, I agree with you there," Holly said. My phone rang then, and I glanced down and saw it was Ben.

"Hi," I greeted.

"Sorry, I was talking to someone else and I had to hit 'ignore' because I couldn't put them on hold. Not that I know how to do that on cell phones."

"That's okay. I don't either."

"So what's the deal?"

"Yeah, we're coming to the movie Sunday. But where are we going?"

"The mainland. We have to meet at Arnold dock."

"Great. What time does the movie start?"

"Seven. So let's meet so we can make the six o'clock ferry."

"Okay. So why did you want to come to church with me?"

"I know a lot of Catholics. I've never been to a Catholic church, and I want to go. Hanging with you makes it perfect."

"But that's not really a reason."

"Actually, it is. But fine. My aunt wants us all to convert. She married a Catholic guy and converted, and now she wants us to also. We have had some really great discussions about the Catholic faith."

"Okay. Are you just going to go with me right after my shift?"

"Yes. I'll show up more towards the end and wait."

"Okay," I said. Holly caught my glance. "I have to go now, Ben. Bye."

"Bye, Maddi." Then he hung up.

"So where are we going to see the movie Sunday?"

"Mainland."

"Do you mean a theater called that or just that we're going to a theater on the mainland?"

"The second one," I answered.

"So why does he want to go to church with you?"

"He said he was considering converting." I felt happy. Another Catholic person!

"Because of you?"

"I don't think I play a part in it. He said something about his aunt."

"Why don't you think you play a part in him wanting to convert?"

"Because that would mean he really loves me and possibly wants to marry me."

"And that's so bad?"

"Holly! I'm seventeen as of yesterday. We're both a little young."

"Okay, okay!"

"Goodnight, Holly."

"You too, Maddi!"

June 19th

Pink Bedroom

Ben said he's considering converting! Yes! I just hope that if he does, he acts with his beliefs too. There's a lot of people who say they're Catholic but don't practice their beliefs at all.

I'm happy. It's a great weekend, even with work in the days. Too bad nothing's happening tomorrow. That would make it even better.

Oh well. I have to go to sleep now.

"You're not doing anything tonight with Ben, are you?" Holly asked me the next morning.

"Of course not. I'm hanging out with you and Mickie."

"Good. We'll both like that."

"I know." I smiled then. "So what are we doing?"

"I think we should watch a movie. Didn't your brother bring his portable DVD player?"

"Yeah, but before we make a plan we should make sure we have the cord to hook it up to the TV, because then we can watch it full screen with popcorn," I suggested.

"Yeah! Mickie can pick the movie. I don't care if we watch some little kid thing."

"Me neither. Little kid movies are usually pretty cool," I replied.

"Hi," I heard a voice say in my ear. I jumped, even though I immediately recognized it. Of course it was Ben. "So do I get a seat?"

"Yes. Right this way," Holly said immediately, making some mark on her hostess stand. Probably her seating chart. I followed them. I might as well.

"You're here early," I remarked.

"Yeah... well, I woke up early and felt like coming to see you."

"Cool. Are you seriously considering converting?" I asked, cutting the small talk.

"Yes."

"Are you sure? Even as a teen, I think you need to go through RCIA. You have to learn a lot of stuff. All the stuff the kids learn, but in way less time. And get baptized and confirmed," I continued.

"Shut up," Ben said. I did, but not because he told me to. He had a look in his eyes, and I'd never seen it before. At least I don't think I had. Come to think of it... I might have when Holly and I were searching for jobs and I saw him. "Yes, I'm seriously considering converting. I don't care if I have to go through all that, and yes, I know what I have to go through. I talked to my aunt. Do you not believe me or something?"

"I'm not sure," I replied, and as I said this I realized that I recognized the look in his eyes. He was determined, that's what it meant. And I had seen it at the Grand Hotel. I guess he had been determined to ask me out.

"Well, believe me, I'm definitely considering it."

"Cool. I should go now," I said.

"See you in a few minutes!" Ben called after me as I left his table. He was right, he would. I had to bring him his Coke. But I couldn't ignore my other customers, so I brought him his pop last and turned to leave. "You're not going to talk? How did I make you mad?" he asked.

"You didn't. But I'm busy. I have to go."

"Okay." Ben let me leave.

"You're acting weird," Holly informed me.

"No, I'm not," I insisted. But just then, Mom, Dad, and Luke walked in with Uncle Chuck, Aunt Annie, and Mickie. Great. My lucky day. "Hi!" I greeted them, plastering on a smile.

"Hi, Maddi," Mickie exclaimed. "We came again!"

"That's true. We used to come here so often and now we haven't been," Mom added.

"Yeah, well, it was the French Outpost when we came here all the time," I pointed out.

"Follow me, please," Holly interrupted. I walked with my customers again.

"Where have you been going for lunch?"

"Yankee Rebel Tavern, Mary's Bistro, and Pink Pony, and we actually made it into the Seabiscuit, but mostly we've been eating at home," Luke answered my question. He wasn't thrilled by that, I could tell. After all, we didn't have chicken at home that was fried. It was his favorite food, although he didn't eat as much of it now that he was trying to eat healthier.

"That makes sense. It would be a lot of money to eat out every lunch for three weeks," I replied. Once they sat down, I said, "Okay, so what do you guys want to drink?"

"Waters all around," Dad said.

"No, I wanted an iced tea with lemon," Mom protested.

"Diet Coke for both of us," Aunt Annie said for her and Uncle Chuck.

"Mommy, can I have pop?" Mickie asked.

"No, just milk or water."

"Okay, I want milk, Maddi."

"Can you mix pop flavors for me?" Luke asked.

"No. I doubt we're allowed to do that anyway."

"Luke, you're getting water," Dad said.

"Fine," Luke pouted.

"Okay. I'll be back soon." I left and walked over to Ben. I was panicking again. "How are you doing?" I asked, faking the cheer.

"What's the problem?" he asked.

"They're here again."

"Who's they?"

"My family," I replied, nearly hyperventilating.

"Oh. Okay. Should I leave or do you want me to stay?"

"Stay. Just, don't do anything obvious," I asked.

"That's fine by me. Oh, hey, can I have a burger?"

"Sure," I said as I left his table yet again. I grabbed a tray and filled glasses for my family.

"Hi again," I greeted them as I walked up and passed out their glasses. "Ready to order?"

"I don't think so. Just a little bit longer," Uncle Chuck said.

"Sure." I walked around my customers making sure everyone was happy, and couldn't help but make my way over to Ben. "Ugh!"

"Maddi, it's okay. It shouldn't be this stressful to have your family come to eat at the restaurant you work at."

"I know. That's why I'm frustrated," I told him. He held my hand and squeezed it, but let go quickly and discreetly. "Okay, I'm going back over." I left without waiting for his answer. He had given me a little courage. "Ready?"

"Yes!" Mickie exclaimed.

"Good. I need my pen," I said. I grabbed it and wrote their orders down. "Okay, I'll go place these for you." I did what I said I would and walked into the inside part of the restaurant. When I came back out, I noticed Aunt Annie was missing from the table. I glanced around hoping she was in the bathroom, but no luck. She was at Ben's table, and I couldn't figure out why. I walked over quietly.

"Why is my niece over here so much?" Aunt Annie was asking. Of course, direct question, no avoidance.

"Who's that?" he asked.

"The waitress," my aunt replied, a little frustrated that he didn't know. From what she knew of him, I didn't see why she thought he should know who she was.

"I'm a needy customer and I tip well," Ben lied.

"No, I don't think that's it. You just have a Coke and you didn't get here after us."

"Yes, but I ordered just a few minutes ago."

"I still don't believe that's it. I think she likes you." I blushed at hearing this. I did.

"Well, I don't know," Ben answered. I chose to interrupt then.

"Hey, Aunt Annie," I smiled. "Why are you over here?"

"Trying to find out if you like him."

"Why would I have told a complete stranger I like him?" I asked. Attacking her common sense to weaken her argument usually worked.

"Because you aren't complete strangers. I don't believe that, either," she said to Ben.

"Well, you're going to have to. Go back to your own table, Aunt Annie," I suggested.

"Fine. Coming over?"

"In a second," I replied. I heard her muttering under her breath, something about how I just proved her theory. "I'm sorry," I apologized to Ben.

"That's okay. She thinks you like me."

"Why would I be dating you if I didn't?"

"No idea. So, yeah, I guess I knew that. But it's still funny."

"Okay, well, since I told her I would…"

"Go."

June 20th

Living Room

Today's work day was stressful. Aunt Annie showed up again and made me stress. She even went over to Ben's table. What's with her sense for these things?

Okay, so currently Holly and I are waiting for Mickie to pick a movie for us to watch. We made the popcorn and it's in a bowl on the table with the puzzle on it. The puzzle is almost finished! Holly and I don't care if Mickie picks a little kid movie, but I hope it's something good. Not "My Little Pony" or anything.

Okay, Mickie picked a movie. Gotta go now.

"Okay. Do you want *Enchanted* or *Alvin and the Chipmunks*?" Mickie asked, bringing Holly and I the two DVDs.

"I don't care," I told her.

"I think we should watch *Enchanted*," Holly said.

"Great. Mickie, go put it in the player."

"Done. Can I sit in between you?" Mickie questioned.

"Of course," Holly replied, sliding over a little on the old faded couch. Mickie sat down between my feet and Holly's legs and positioned herself like I was. Then she leaned into my side. The menu came on after the previews.

"Oops. I forgot to push play!" Mickie jumped up to push play, seeing as we didn't have the remote to the portable player. She came to sit back down, exactly like she was before.

The movie seemed to pass quickly. But the popcorn disappeared faster. We refilled the bowl three times. And I was about to get up and refill it again, but Holly's glance froze me.

"What, Holly? Why do you keep looking at me?" I asked, a little peeved.

"I can't make fun of this movie with Mickie," Holly replied.

"What is there to make fun of in *Enchanted*?" Mickie jumped up then, protesting. "Are you going to fight?" she questioned. "I don't want you to make fun of the movie. But I don't want you to fight anymore."

"No, we won't fight, Mickie," Holly comforted her.

"Yeah. Sorry, Holly. I'm not feeling the best. Maybe I'm just tired," I suggested. Or I'm frustrated. Spending all this time together doesn't work sometimes."

"It's fine. I know. We're all stressed, and I know what you had to deal with today."

"Okay. Thanks," I said. "I'll go get more popcorn."

"Okay. Can we rewind?" Mickie asked.

"No," I called from the kitchen a few feet away. "The remote is missing. You can try scene selections, if you want."

"Yes. Holly, can you help me?" I heard Holly get up to help and I came back a few minutes later.

"Can we finish the movie now?" I asked.

"Yes!" Mickie exclaimed, pressing play. We all settled down again until it was over. Mickie ended up falling asleep in my lap before the movie ended. I managed to carry her upstairs and got her tucked into bed. Then Holly and I got ready for bed and grabbed our books for a little reading before going to sleep. It was a good night.

Devon Warriner   ----------   Get Over it

June 21ˢᵗ

Gate House bathroom

Where is Ben? Mass starts at 5:30! And I get off work at 5:00. Yeah, we have some time. But not a lot. I mean, we have to walk down there, seeing as Holly and I walked to work today.

It's 5:15, and I'm already changed for church. It's not really nice like I would wear for church at home, but it's not my work uniform. Just nice denim Capri's and a top. But come on! This is making me impatient!

"Holly, he's late! We have to leave soon to make it to church."

"What if he doesn't come in time to make it?" she asked.

"If he doesn't make it here in five minutes, I'm walking down. Can you wait five minutes after that and tell him if you see him that I'm waiting?"

"Sure. Of course, Maddi," Holly replied. She had barely said this when Ben got to the gate.

"Hey, Ben," I greeted as he stopped. "Church starts in around ten minutes, so we have to go now," I told him. "Bye, Holly! You're going home, right?"

"Yeah. I'm going home. There's no point in hanging out downtown. See you there," she replied.

"Yeah, bye!" I said, giving her a hug. Then I turned to Ben. "Okay, let's go."

"This is called the Gospel. And we all have to stand," I whispered, pulling Ben up from his seat. "And then in a few minutes is the Homily. We just sit and listen."

"You don't have to educate me on the ways of the Church," Ben said. "I just want to see a Mass and what I think of it. And enjoy it, if I can. With you. If you're trying to teach me all this stuff, neither of us are relaxed, and it's no fun."

"I guess not," I replied. "But it's not having fun that's the reason I go to church, either." People were beginning to notice our whispered conversation. The lady in front of me turned and glared. "Okay, just listen now."

"I was until you started talking," he replied.

I smiled. "Whatever."

After Mass, we headed for the front doors of the church and shook the priest's hand on the way out. Standing on the front porch of the church holding Ben's hand just felt right. Ben had seemed really comfortable in church.

"So, did you *enjoy* Mass?" I asked.

"Yes, actually."

"Are you converting?"

"I already was going to."

"That's awesome!" I exclaimed.

"Yeah, I wondered what your reaction would be. Can I walk you home?" he asked.

"Of course." We started walking back to Dufina.

"So, are you really into Catholicism?"

"Into it as in what?"

"I don't know. Answer the question."

"Well, I'm not into it like I'm going to become a nun. I probably couldn't handle that. But I'm really into following my beliefs. And I'm mad when people are supposedly Catholic but make decisions leaving their Catholic beliefs out of it."

"Like what?"

"Voting for pro-choice candidates to be in office. Any office at all. Actually, voting for almost any liberal agenda."

"Whoa. You're like, extremist in your views."

"Yeah, but not so much that I'll assassinate the president if they end up being a liberal."

"Do you wish you could vote now?"

"I wished I could vote when I was thirteen years old."

"Extremist," he muttered.

"No, I'm really not. Listen to some other conservatives. They're worse. Why? What do you think?"

"If they could do better for the economy than a conservative Republican, I'd vote for the Democrat."

"Okay. You're old enough to vote this year. Who are you voting for?"

"It's June. I don't know who's on the ballot."

"As it stands right now. Pick one."

"I don't know. Obama or Clinton."

"Ugh! That makes me sick."

"You want to break up?" he offered.

"Oh. Don't tempt me."

"You know everyone doesn't have to have the same views you do," he replied.

"I know. I've been told that for four years. I understand they don't have to, I just wish they did."

"Okay. Maybe, if you convince me, I'll change my mind and vote for a conservative."

"Which one?" I asked, curious.

"Whichever one's on the ballot."

"Good. I look forward to more of this argument. I know I'll win," I gloated as we came to the "driveway" of Dufina.

"Whatever," he muttered.

"Nice comeback. You know I'll end up winning."

"Maybe. Goodnight, crazy extremist lady," Ben said. He went to kiss me, but I stopped him.

"Goodnight insane Democrat," I tried. Then I reached up to kiss him. But *he* stopped *me*.

"Nah, doesn't sound as good."

"Oh, whatever. Kiss me already!" I told him. So he did.

"Goodnight," I told him when we broke apart.

"See you later, Maddi." I walked away feeling giddy and smiling.

June 21st

Pink Bedroom

    Oh my gosh. Today was a great day. I got to talk politics. And I love arguing with Democrats. But it's hard to do with my friends who don't even try to understand what I'm saying. Oh, wait, I do that too. I'll try to understand, but I'll never change my opinion on this.

    And I'm still really glad Ben is converting. I mean, a lot of people don't go to church anymore, and not many convert, so it's cool when someone does.

    Okay, I have to tell Holly what happened today, so I gotta go.

"Hey, Ben," I greeted my boyfriend as I walked up to his table. There were two others with him. I was disappointed. I couldn't convince him to change his views with company. It'd have to wait until tomorrow.

"Hi, Maddi. This is Nick and that's Anna. They wanted to come with me today." I glanced over at them while he was talking. Nick had dark hair and green eyes, a broad nose, and long eyelashes. Anna had sandy brown hair with very pretty blue eyes. I was biased, true, but I didn't think they were as beautiful as Ben's. Anna's were an amazing shade, though. She had a thin nose, small ears, and her lips were small and pink.

"Hi, Maddi," Anna said.

"So how do you all know – I mean, what do you want to drink?" I asked as I noticed Mr. Poe staring at me. He was still such a creep!

"Coke," Ben replied.

"Coke, and buffalo wings," Nick said.

"Do you have Cherry Coke? I'm guessing you were going to ask how we knew Ben." Here she paused, waiting for my nod. "We work with him every summer," Anna answered helpfully.

"But you're here every day," I said to Ben.

"Our jobs don't start until July. They're here early because it's so beautiful."

"That's cool," I said. "I better get back to work. But when I come back, tell me where you work." I smiled at them, but an obvious false smile that told them I didn't want to work.

"We can always make it interesting," Ben suggested, reading my expression perfectly.

"I'd rather you not. I don't know what you're thinking, but I don't believe it's a good idea," I told him warily. I turned to leave again, and this time he let me. I was so glad that they were the only ones here. I loved days like this when nothing was happening. I got their drinks and returned. They were laughing at something, so I dropped off the cups and went over to Holly. They had made her permanent hostess, as she was so good at it and someone had quit.

"Are you jealous?" she asked me. She knew me too well.

"No," I lied.

"Then why aren't you hanging out over *there*?"

"Because you're all alone *here*," I replied truthfully. "And she so does not like him! Does she?"

"Well..." We both stared at the group of three for a while. Anna noticed me staring, shot me a look, and took Nick's hand. I liked Anna so much. It seemed like she could read my mind. Ben followed her gaze and motioned me over.

"Come on, Maddi, hang out over here," Ben said, taking my hand when I was in reach and pulling me closer. I jerked my hand away, in case the creep was watching. At least, that was what I told myself.

"But Holly's all alone."

"And no one's here. Ask if you guys can come sit down with us." I knew Ben was right, and I was cornered, no way to get out of it.

"Fine," I sighed, a little frightened. "Mr. Poe, nobody's here, so Holly and I were wondering if we could sit and hang out with our friends who are."

"Fine," he said, slightly angry. I was surprised. Was he mad at me? But I motioned to Holly, and she went with me to Ben's table.

"So... Maddi," Anna started to speak after Holly and I were finished dragging our chairs to the table, "you're going out with Ben?"

"Yes." Ben leaned over to kiss me to prove it, but I moved over away from him more. "What's with you today, Maddi?" he asked. I could understand why. I wasn't acting normal. But I couldn't lose my job. Again, that's what I convinced myself of.

"Creepy is watching, more than he usually does, because we're the only ones here."

"Oh. Wait. Who's Creepy?" Nick asked.

"The manager. He has an insane amount of rules. The last one is 'No PDA', which is just stupid."

"Yeah, I agree," Anna put in.

"What's PDA?" Nick questioned.

"Public displays of affection," I replied. "Oh, did you want anything besides the appetizer?" I asked, switching modes.

"No, we ate lunch. We just came to hang out," Ben said.

"Okay."

"You know, we don't have it yet," Nick hinted.

"Oh!" Holly jumped up, saying she'd get it. Ben kissed me quickly as Holly said something to Mr. Poe. Then I realized they hadn't answered my question.

"Where do you guys work?" I asked.

"On Arnold ferries," Anna replied.

"Sometimes we're on different ferries, but we're usually on the same boat," Nick continued.

"How did you get that?" I asked. Nick and Anna shot Ben a look, and he made a face back.

"Well, my family owns Arnold Transit Company," Ben started. "That's why we live on the island."

"Seriously?" Holly shrieked.

"Is that how you can come to the restaurant almost every day?" I asked.

"Yup."

"Shouldn't your name be Arnold? I mean last?"

"No. My mom's family started it. And so my name is different."

"You look upset," Anna pointed out.

"I am a little. But I think it's cool," I told her, hiding my thoughts. I was upset. Why hadn't Ben told me. It wasn't like *I* was keeping any major secrets from *him*. Ben looked relieved. "But how come you didn't tell me?"

"I didn't want you to like me for money," Ben told me.

"I'm not that kind of girl," I said.

"I know that, Maddi." Nick elbowed Ben, who said, "I'm sorry."

"That's okay. It's cool that you guys own it," I replied.

* * *

"Maddi, will you clean up that table?" Mr. Poe asked, pointing to Ben's usual table.

"Sure." I went over there and grabbed the cups and plates and put them on my tray. I picked up the garbage too, but I noticed there was writing on a napkin. It was none of my business and it could have hurt me. After all, I really didn't know anything about Nick and Anna or if they actually like me or not. I read it anyway.

I love you, Maddi.
- Ben

I experienced a new happy, with my heart light and giggles almost tumbling out. I folded up the napkin and put it in my pocket, trying to stop my grin. I was really happy I was going out with Ben tonight. Holly was helping me by saying we were going out to dinner. But we were taking a ferry to the mainland with Ben and seeing a movie. I was floating on air for the rest of my shift.

Devon Warriner   ----------   Get Over it

June 22nd
Pink Bedroom

Oh! My! Gosh! Ben just said he loved me! Well, he didn't say it, he wrote it, but still. I'm so happy! I don't think I heard anything Holly said on the way home.

Ben

+

Maddi

I love him too. He's amazing. Funny. Cute (or hot, if I was like other girls). I don't say "hot." It's weird. But anyway, just... oh my gosh! I might squeal!

I had the biggest smile on my face when we met Ben at the Arnold dock. It was cool that his family owned it.

"Maddi, you're like, insane," Holly said. I hadn't told her what Ben said yet, but I was frantically searching for him. I finally found him, and he smiled too. I ran up to hug him.

"I love you too," I whispered in his ear before I pulled back to kiss him. Holly cleared her throat. "Sorry, Holls," I said a couple seconds later. I couldn't come down from my cloud. Meaning I was still smiling like a maniac.

"Let's go," Ben suggested. He took my hand and pulled me down the dock. Holly followed.

"Hey, um… Since Holly's coming with us, we can't make her feel like a third wheel. Like, no cliché movie watching. Okay? I know how much you love clichés."

"Which means?"

"No kissing throughout the whole movie," I whispered. I let go of his hand when he said that was okay and slowed to walk by Holly. "So Ben told me he loves me today," I said happily.

"Yeah, I thought so. I mean, that's great!" Holly replied with false enthusiasm coloring her voice.

"What do you mean?"

"You've been distracted all day, and you're *still* smiling. I'm happy for you, but it was obvious."

"Obvious enough for Aunt Annie to know?" I was worried now. "She always wants to know," I moaned. I started to hyperventilate, and I stopped dead in my tracks. Ben stopped and came back to me.

"What's the matter?" he asked. I couldn't speak, couldn't get sound to come through my lips.

"She doesn't want anyone to know she has a boyfriend, but she thinks her gossipy aunt knows," Holly answered for me.

"It's okay," Ben reassured me, rubbing my back. He kissed my cheek. I was crying at this point. Holly gave me a hug, and together they made me stop.

"Do you still want to go to the movie?" Ben asked.

"Yes," I replied. Yes, I was definitely way below cloud nine now. But maybe I could get back there again.

Devon Warriner   ----------   Get Over it

June 22nd

Pink Bedroom

Okay, it's typical to write in a journal once a day. Well, if I did that, my journal would take up maybe three lines. I'd forget everything. And I do not want to forget anything about Ben or my trip here this year.

We went to the movie, as planned. I guess I was still crying, because when I sat up from leaning on Ben's shoulder, his blue shirt (which matched his eyes) was a darker color, and also damp. Holly kept making comments about the movie — enough to make me laugh. She's an amazing friend.

Ben's amazing too. A normal guy would have been offended if they heard their girlfriend didn't want people to know about them, right? But Ben wasn't.

Why wasn't he? I'm confused now!

"Hello?"

"Why didn't you react when Holly said that?"

"Said what?"

"That I didn't want anyone to know I was going out with you," I replied.

"Because," Ben answered.

"Do you know why not?"

"No."

"Because my aunt would tell everyone she knows, and I don't want her to do that. Actually, she'd probably hire a skywriter and have him write 'Maddi Andrews has a boyfriend!' back home."

"Oh."

"Are you mad?" I asked, worried.

"A little."

"I'm sorry," I said. What else could I do? " I love you."

"Love you, too."

"Okay. Bye, then." I almost cried.

"Yup. Bye," Ben replied. I sat on my bed for a minute, my phone still up to my ear, hearing nothing.

"Maddi! What's wrong?" Holly asked me. Huh. I hadn't heard or seen her come in the room. My tears burst out, crushing my will.

"He'll probably break up with me now!" I sobbed. Holly came and gave me a hug.

"Why?"

"Because I'm ashamed of him, he thinks."

"Is that my fault?" Holly questioned.

"No. It's definitely not," I replied.

"Okay. Hon, it's late. Go to sleep. You'll feel better tomorrow," Holly suggested.

"Maybe," I balked.

"Sleep," she insisted softly.

"Okay. Goodnight, Holly."

"Night, Maddi."

* * *

"Holly, how did I get here?" I asked in a daze.

"You mean to work? Like normal, on your bike. You don't remember?"

"No."

"You were dazed, true, but I didn't know it was that much," Holly said. I didn't reply. "Maddi, you need to take a break. Go ask Mr. Poe." I followed Holly's directions and asked.

He immediately replied, "Ten minutes." So I went and sat down, not paying any attention to what I was doing. But five minutes into my break I was freaking out. What if Ben showed up? What if he didn't? What did it mean if he didn't? I could have gotten up to look, but I was afraid to. Slowly, the rest of my break passed. I ran outside when my break was over, knowing I would have to anyway, looking for Ben. Would he have shown up? Ah! There he was! I ran up to him and tried to kiss him, but he stopped me. No!

"What's wrong?" I asked, worried.

"Maddi, I really do love you," he started. Uh-oh! Break-up words! "But you said you loved me too, and were really upset when you thought your aunt knew. I knew you did it before, but this was more." Great. I don't even get the "It's not you, it's me" line. At least he was truthful. And man enough to break up in person.

"Yeah, but she doesn't, so everything's fine!" I tried.

"It's not. If you're ashamed to be with me, why don't you admit it and break it off?" Ben looked at me sadly, like he didn't want this to happen too. If he didn't want this to happen though, why was he doing it?

"But I'm not ashamed..." I started.

"Really? Because it seems like you are. And I can't do this."

"You're seriously breaking up with me?" I asked as my heart broke, willing it to be a lie.

"Would I joke about it?" I started to cry as he spoke but hid my tears. His words were too harsh. "Yes, seriously! Goodbye, Maddi," Ben said. Then he turned around and left. I wiped away the tears that had already come as Mr. Poe walked up, but it was hard to stifle the urge to throw something. I know from my first crush that I was more of an anger person than a sobbing person. I mean, in eighth grade, as soon as I found out my first crush had a girlfriend, I wanted to yell, and I didn't cry.

"I could have you fired for neglecting your customers!" he yelled. I wanted to roll my eyes - become a sarcastic brat who nobody said anything mean to because they knew something was making them upset - but I resisted. "But I won't fire you today. You don't look good." Oh my gosh! Creepy had a heart! I went around to all my customers after he left, barely managing to put on a smile. But one customer noticed my black cloud.

"Sugar, are y'all right?" a somewhat elderly southern woman asked me as I came to her table.

"Yeah, fine," I said. Thankfully, my shift was almost over.

"All right, then. But y'all can talk to me if y'alls want!" she offered.

"No, really, I'm fine," I insisted. I completed her and her husband's orders, left them, and glanced at my watch. Yes! 5:00!

"Happy birthday, Aunt Annie!" I was faking the enthusiasm in both my voice and expression. It was good that I could act. Aunt Annie was smiling and staring at the cake I had made for her. It was double chocolate- the cake and frosting, and I had written "Happy Birthday" in yellow gel. It actually hadn't taken very long.

"Happy birthday to you," Mom started singing, so I set the cake down.

"Wait. Where are the candles?" Aunt Annie asked.

"There are none. I didn't have any either," I informed her.

"Oh. Go on," she replied.

"Sheesh. Are you a little kid?" I was a little annoyed.

"At forty-five? Yes! And I'm proud." Aunt Annie and my mother were very similar in their little kid behavior.

"Okay," my mom interrupted, then started singing again. Everyone did except for me. I only mouthed the words. Holly, who was next to me, nudged me until I glared at her. She stopped, confused. I had forgotten that I hadn't told her.

After we were done singing, Aunt Annie cut the cake and we devoured it. Holly and I were done after Luke and Mickie were. Being the youngest, they ate fastest.

"Excuse us," Holly said, pulling me upstairs. "Okay, you're telling me now. What's wrong?" I stared at her, telling myself not to cry.

"Well... Ben broke up with me," I hesitantly admitted. Holly looked at me all sad-like. I broke down and let out a sob, and Holly gave me a long hug.

"I'm sorry. I know you really liked him."

"No, actually, I love him. But it's okay. I'll get over it. I know I will," I said as soon as I could speak in sentences again.

"Do you need to cry?" I looked at Holly like she was crazy. What did she think I had been doing? But I realized I hadn't been crying, just started to.

"No. I don't really cry about things like this. I only get mad."

"Do you need to scream?"

"Nope. I'll bottle it up until it comes out in tears. That'd be quieter."

"It may be quieter, but it's not healthy for you. Stress and all that."

"I don't care. Can we quit talking about it?"

"Sure. Let's go back downstairs," Holly suggested.

"Good." When we got back downstairs, Aunt Annie had started opening presents. Weird, I didn't think we took that long. But whatever.

Devon Warriner ---------- Get Over it

June 24th
Pink Bedroom

    I miss him already! And it hasn't even been 24 hours since he broke up with me. I don't want to be that kind of girl who pathetically spends the whole next day crying, especially because that would confuse my family members. And I don't want to be the girl that calls her ex asking to take her back. I won't be pathetic! Great. I need Holly's help for that.

    Hmm... It's not my day off, so it's slightly easier. But I wonder if Holly and I could do stuff after work... if my family would mind us "going out for dinner" again in the same week. We could eat, then bike around the island, come back... I don't know. I have to talk to Holly. Why is she always up before me now?

"Hey, Holly. If it's okay with my family, do you mind eating out for dinner, just the two of us, and riding our bikes around the island?" I asked.

"I don't know," Holly replied. I made my best puppy dog face, which wasn't that good, but still succeeded. Probably because she felt sorry for me. I felt like sticking my tongue out, but she wouldn't have understood.

"Thanks. I'm going to go ask Mom if it's okay," I told her. So I went in search for Mom, and found her a few minutes later in the living room. "Hey, Mom?"

"What, sweetheart?"

"Well, Holly and I were wondering if we could skip family dinner again. Go out just the two of us, and bike around the island. Because we're missing out on that stuff while we're working."

"Didn't you just go out Sunday night? And what about your days off?"

"We've been doing everything else on our days off. And yes, we did. But we were hoping we could do it again."

Mom sighed. "Sure. Go tell Mickie. She'll probably be disappointed, and I'm sure no one else wants to tell her."

I smiled with victory. "Okay. Thanks, Mom." I gave her a hug before I left to find Mickie. Telling her didn't go as well as getting my mom to agree, but it wasn't full on waterworks and screaming disappointment. Just a pouty lip, puppy dog eyes, and a soft voice pleading for us to stay. "I'm sorry, Mickie. But we both really want to go. Remember, tomorrow is my day off, and I can hang with you for half the day."

"Okay," she agreed.

"Thanks for understanding, Mick. You're the best!" Mickie's face lit up at this comment, and I almost laughed as I left her to go to work. "We're all good, Holly. Let's go."

"We're taking our bikes, right?" she teased.

"Yes!" I exclaimed, then rolled my eyes, going along with it.

"Look at you. Stay this way. It's better than any moping attitude," Holly remarked. My eyes teared. Great. A preview of my day today. "Oops. Sorry. I won't comment on it anymore," Holly said when she realized I was suddenly upset.

"It's okay. I'm fine," I assured her.

"I know. Come on, let's go, honey." We hopped on our bikes and left with a great day ahead of us… yeah, right.

"Welcome to the Gate House. My name's Maddi, and I'll be your server today. Do you know what you want to drink yet?" I asked. My fake smile was plastered on my face.

"Diet Pepsi," the man in the red shirt said.

"Me too," his wife agreed.

"I'm sorry, we have Coke products," I started.

"Then Diet Coke," the man snapped. I was sure my face fell then, so I worked my smiling muscles more to make sure I was smiling.

"Okay. You too?" I asked his wife.

"Yes, please," she replied.

"Okay. I'll go get those for you," I told them, but then went over to talk to Holly. "They have no manners!" I exclaimed. "I don't want to deal with them!"

"I'm sorry. I had to seat them in your section. No tables in Laura's or Sara's sections were available."

"That's okay. I know you wouldn't do that unless you had to. But I gotta go get their drinks," I said. "See you in a bit." So I left to get the drinks. I put the cups under the dispensers, pressed the button, and waited. I headed outside to bring the cups to the couple, but started crying as I spotted a table another couple was now sitting at. Holly saw me and threw a weak smile my way. I told myself to breathe and smile, and then gave the drinks to the first couple. Then I walked over to what was once Ben's table with my heart heavy and greeted the couple. See? An amazing day.

"Are we going biking or eating first?" Holly asked after we were released and changed from our work uniform.

"Well, sunset's late. After nine. I don't think it matters," I said.

"Let's eat first," she suggested.

"But it doesn't take a really long time to bike around the island since we're both in shape. And if we go biking first, most of the day tourists will be gone and restaurants will be way less busy that late," I countered.

"Okay... If we go biking first, let's try to go to the Seabiscuit Café for dinner."

"Sounds good to me."

"Okay. Let's go!"

We quickly made it from the Gate House to the Star Line Ferry Dock side of downtown and headed west on the outer road. We always went around the island that way, which was the opposite way most people seemed to. The direction you went around the island didn't matter at all, we just liked going the other way. The water looked beautiful, as always, and the trees on the inside of the road looked pretty also. This was part of the reason I loved Mackinac Island. It was peaceful and pretty.

"Hey, Holly! Do you want to stop at British Landing?" I asked when we were coming close to it.

"No. Let's keep going!" she called back.

"Got it." Talking was hard as we biked, even when we were right next to each other. It wasn't that it was windy or that something was really noisy. It was just more fun to bike in company but keep to your own thoughts. Relaxing. Peaceful. Just what I needed. And Holly knew it. She was just awesome like that.

June 24th

Family Room

Holly was great today. She knew what I felt and what I didn't want to do. It seemed like she could read my mind. Apparently a lot of people can do that. I'm just predictable. Anyway…

I'm thinking that Holly, Mickie, and I should go bowling tomorrow at the Woods Golf Course Restaurant. It'd be a fun thing to do. Almost five-year-olds can bowl, right? It's just duckpin bowling, and the ball is small and seemingly light… My friends and I bowled when I turned six, so some of them were five… I don't know. I'll ask Aunt Annie and see what she says. And if she doesn't know, either she or I could call her aunt, who took Luke a long time ago to the bowling alley.

I'll figure this out tomorrow. It's 10:30 (wow, kind of early) and I'm tired.

"Hey, Aunt Annie?"

"What, Maddi?"

"Do you think Mickie could go bowling with Holly and me?"

"Do you mean can she go or can she do it?"

"Could she do it."

"Probably. And if not, she can always watch you and Holly."

"Okay. Now I'm asking if she can go."

"Of course. She's been begging to hang out with you since you took that job."

"Great! I'll go tell her. And Holly. See you later, Aunt Annie!"

"So we're going bowling?" Holly asked when I crashed into her leaving the kitchen.

"Yup. Is that okay?"

"It sounds fun!"

"It's an old fashioned kind of bowling and we even have to reset the pins."

"It still sounds fun. Are you trying to get me to not go?"

"No. I'm just making sure you know everything about it."

"I got it. I'm fine."

"What's fine?" Mickie asked.

"The kitchen is apparently the meeting place this morning," I pointed out.

"Well, it's morning. Everyone's hungry," Holly said.

"That's true. We're going bowling this morning, Mickie," I told her. Mickie's face fell and a pout began to form. "You're coming with us. Then we're coming back here for lunch, and dropping you off."

"I can't hang out with you more than that?" Mickie questioned.

"Maybe," Holly said.

"Okay. Are we going yet?"

"No. Have you eaten breakfast?" I laughed.

"Yes," she replied.

"Oh. Well, Holly and I haven't."

"I ate, too," Holly admitted.

"Fine. We'll leave after I'm done eating," I told them. They laughed, and I rolled my eyes and poured my cereal.

"Spare!" I exclaimed when Mickie knocked down all the pins on her second try that turn. "I think you fixed the tilt in the floor."

"There's a tilt in the floor?" she asked.

"It seems like it. We've never gotten a spare the whole time we've been here."

"The whole twenty minutes?" Holly asked.

"Yes!"

"I'll go reset them!" Mickie volunteered. She ran up the hallway to reset the pins. The hallway of this bowling alley was long and narrow, with spring green walls. They were like the crayon color with a little less yellow. The halls were lined with picture frames. The frames all had red, white, and blue ribbons in them. The pins were really small duckpins, not even as long as my forearm, and the balls were small and brown or green and about as big as a croquet ball.

"It's your turn, Holly," I said, nudging her forward.

"Okay." She took the ball from my hand, and rolled it down the lane. It fell into the gutter.

"Oh, well. Mickie! We need you to fix the floor again!" I called.

"What?"

"Just kidding, Mick." Holly threw the ball again, this time knocking down about half the pins.

"Six!" Mickie called out. Then she reset the pins and threw the balls back down. Next it was my turn.

"Three!" Mickie called out. My next ball landed in the gutter. And our game went on until 11:30, when we got tired. It was mostly a low-scoring game, not that we kept real track of points. We just remembered never getting a strike, barely any spares, and usually not much over half the pins. It was a fun game, especially towards the end when we started setting up the pins in different shapes.

"Okay, let's get walking. It takes a bit to get from here to Dufina, and I'm hungry," I suggested. "Not to sound bossy. Sorry if I did."

"You weren't bossy," Holly spoke at the same time as Mickie.

"I'm hungry too!" Mickie exclaimed.

"Did you have fun today?" I asked Holly as we walked downtown for what seemed like the millionth time in June.

"Yeah. Of course."

"Good."

"You sound like my mom."

"Oh. Sorry," I apologized.

"You don't have to apologize, it just seems funny."

"Okay. So where do you want to go?"

"Well, let's act like tourists and go shopping more."

"You want to go shopping *more*? You went shopping a lot already."

"So? Let's go to that huge store," Holly suggested.

"The Big Store with the Little Prices?"

"Yeah, that one."

"Why?" I asked.

"So I can buy gifts for my family."

"Okay, sure, we can go there." It didn't take us very long to reach that particular store in the middle of downtown.

"Ooh! Look at this snow globe!" Holly exclaimed. It had the Mackinac bridge and a ferry in the actual globe, and cartoon-y places on the island on the base.

"Yeah, if you're buying a snow globe here, you should buy that one. Every other one is plastic and cheap," I said, pointing out an arc-shaped "snow globe" with the bridge, a boat, the lighthouse, and a horse-drawn carriage on the plastic sitting in the middle. "You know, Edward's Gifts has nicer snow globes. I know there's one with a gazebo in the middle and pretty scenes on the base."

"Yeah, but where is there a fancy gazebo on the island?"

"The gazebo is near the Fort and the East Bluff. It's hard to find unless you read the signs. It's used for a lot of weddings and was made for the movie *Somewhere in Time*," I answered.

"Well, I'm buying this one," Holly told me.

"Okay. Now what?"

"Visors or hats? T-shirts? Both? I don't know. You go look at shirts. I'm going to look at hats," Holly directed. I quickly picked the two best shirts I could find and brought them to Holly.

"Which one? Or either of them?" I asked.

"Both," she said, grabbing them and throwing them over her arm. "Which one?" she questioned, first pointing to a green visor that would only fit her sister, and then a pink hat that could be for either her sister or mother.

"Um."

"You're right. I'll get both," she decided. Then she grabbed a hat for her dad and headed to the cash register.

"Wow. You *really* love shopping."

"No, actually not so much. I love being a tourist and doing the tourist shopping."

"Oh. Okay. 'Cause there's such a big difference," I said sarcastically. Holly looked at my expression and laughed.

"You hate tourist shopping, don't you?"

"Not really," I lied.

"You don't lie very well," Holly told me. "I'm done. We can go back to the cottage, if you want."

"And do what?" I asked.

"Gossip? I don't know. We can always call Emily, work on the puzzle, or watch TV if we're entirely bored."

"Okay. Sounds good," I said. "But we should go to the Butterfly House first. It's really cool... I mean, hot, but it's amazing to see all the beautiful butterflies *and* the flowers."

"No problem. We should both have fun today."

"I love you, Holly."
"I know." She smiled and I rolled my eyes.

As we came up Annex Road I saw a figure at the end of the Dufina driveway. "Holly!" I whispered. "Is that who I think it is?" My chest started to ache. I didn't want to see him again, it hurt too much. Why was he standing there?

"Who?" she asked, squinting to see who it was.

"Ben!" As soon as I said his name, my heart broke a second time.

"Oh. I don't know. Come on," she said, pulling me beside her. It *was* who I thought it was. "Hi, Ben," Holly greeted curtly. I smiled a little.

"Hi, Holly," Ben said, his voice friendly but soft.

"What do you want?" Holly asked.

"Maddi?" Ben asked. He sounded a little desperate. Which didn't make much sense. But I was going to start crying. I just knew it.

"What?" I managed to get out.

"I want you back," he told me. My attitude and my heart melted right then. I really *was* going to cry, but I knew I had to stay tough and not cry or accept right away. If I cried he would know I wanted him too. If I accepted too soon, same situation. And as much as it was true, I wasn't going to let him know that. Holly would have said it was stupid if she could have read my mind, but I didn't care.

"Why?" I questioned.

"Because I miss you, Maddi!"

"Oh," was the only word I could get out of my mouth.

"Please take me back? I'm sorry I broke up with you."

"You dumped me," I accused.

"Yeah, I guess I did. And I'm sorry. Please?"

"You're begging?" I asked, surprised, but secretly happy. He missed me as much as I missed him. It felt kind of good.

"Yes."

"Okay. But only if you follow me in the house right now."

"Why?" he asked.

"Just follow. You coming, Holly?"

"Yup," was the quick reply I got from Holly.

"Okay. Wait here," I told Ben. "Aunt Annie?" I called after I stepped in the house. Holly followed and called too, her mind reading ability back and working. She obviously couldn't read minds, but sometimes she knew exactly what I was thinking. As was the case here.

"You don't have to do this, Maddi," Ben said, finally understanding what I meant to do.

"Yes, I do. Or it will happen again."

"Okay." My whole family had assembled even though I had just called Annie. For once Dad wasn't out biking. That was just as well. My parents really should have met him first.

"What, Maddi?" Aunt Annie asked. "Mickie was just going to bed."

"Mom, Dad, Aunt Annie, I'd like you to meet Ben." Annie's face lit up like lights on a Christmas tree.

"Hi, Ben," she greeted eagerly.

"Hi, Mrs. ...?"

"Just call me Annie," she told him.

"Okay," he agreed.

"Ben is my boyfriend." Aunt Annie's smile grew wider.

"It's very nice to meet you, Ben."

"You too."

"This is my Mom and Dad," I told him.

"Nice to meet you, Mr. and Mrs. Andrews."

"You too. How are you?" Dad asked.

"Pretty good. And you?"

"I'm good," he replied.

"Okay, that's it. We're leaving now," I interrupted.

"You're leaving the house at eight-thirty?" Holly and Mom asked.

"No. I'm going to say goodbye, then coming back."

"Oh. Okay. See you in a bit," Holly replied. Aunt Annie reluctantly let us go. I laughed and Ben laughed with me as we walked into the backyard filled with its closed-up mini daisies.

"Now do you see why I didn't tell her?"

"Come on, she wasn't that bad," Ben said.

"You're right. That was mild. But she was really excited and probably would have asked you a million questions if we hadn't left or I hadn't been there."

"Maybe. I don't know your aunt's behavior."

"I know. You just met her."

"Really?" he asked. "Okay, just kidding. Goodnight, Maddi."

"Night, Ben." Then he kissed me and walked away. "Bye," I whispered. I was reluctant to go back inside because I knew I would get pounded with questions. But inside I went anyway. I could handle the questions and not get stressed. I had a really great day, with no other stress, so I was willing to give it a shot.

June 26th

Breakfast Room

    I don't want to go back to work this morning. Yesterday was such a great day, like a normal vacation day should be. Going back to work means being stressed by people. Okay, maybe now I have Ben back, so I won't melt down, but I still don't want the stress. People aren't always great.

    I was right about last night. Aunt Annie pestered me with thousands of questions. Other family members did too. Luke even asked a few. But I was asked about all kinds of personal stuff, along with what kinds of things he likes. Mom and Aunt Annie teased me by singing show tunes and songs that have the word "love" in it. ***Sometimes*** it was funny.

    Well... gotta go finish getting ready for work.

"Hello, Mr. Poe," I greeted the manager as we arrived at work. "I just wanted to make sure you remembered that tomorrow is our last day working here. We're leaving on Monday, and we need the weekend to get ready to leave."

"You need two days to pack?"

"Well, no," I admitted.

"Can you please work Saturday?" Mr. Poe asked.

"Well…"

"Yes," Holly replied.

"Good," Mr. Poe said. Holly and I walked away.

"Why?" I asked.

"We get two full weeks of pay that way. You get another full day of tips. And did you have something planned for Saturday?"

"No, but I was hoping to have a few days to ourselves."

"Sorry. You've still got Sunday." Of course Holly would look on the bright side.

"Okay, fine."

"Good. But come on, it's almost eleven."

"You're the one who has to be in place at eleven. I don't."

"Well, come with me to the front," Holly commanded.

"Yes, Your Highness," I joked. Holly just shot me a look. "Sorry."

"Guess what I just got tipped," I said as I came to talk to Holly.

"Three thousand dollars?"

"Nope. Close, though," I laughed. "Three bucks. That's it!"

"Are they behaving well?" she asked.

"What?"

"The bucks."

"Oh. Sure. Whatever."

"You're distracted," Holly pointed out.

"Yup."

"Ben's not here yet?"

"Nope."

"Relax. He will be. Otherwise he wouldn't have begged you to take him back."

"Whatever."

"Maddi!" she exclaimed, frustrated.

"Hi," I heard someone say while I was still staring at Holly. Wait. I knew that voice. I glanced up.

"Hey, Ben."

"Hi, Maddi. Holly, I'd like to sit in Sara's section today?" he laughed.

"Not funny," I mumbled, sulking now.

"Okay. I'm sorry," he apologized.

"That would only be funny if she broke up with you because she thought you were cheating on her with Sara," Holly remarked as she led him to his usual table.

"I apologized. Do you want more?"

"Yes. An all expenses paid trip from you to Hawaii so I can find a better guy," I teased.

"Enough. I get it. Why Hawaii?"

"Because I'd love a vacation there. And I *do* like island boys."

"Oh. Maybe someday," he suggested, kissing me. I rolled my eyes and left to get him a Coke. "Hey, Maddi? Can I get buffalo wings, too?" he asked.

"Sure," I said without turning around.

"I love you." I turned around then.

"Because of the food?" I accused.

"No! I really do."

"I know. I was teasing."

"Yeesh."

"So tomorrow is your last day of work?" Mom asked at dinner, as we all sat around eating the pizza she made.

"No, actually, Holly and Mr. Poe roped me into working Saturday, too," I told her. Then I said to Holly, "You might be a workaholic when you're older."

"Yeah, right. I enjoy the company of my friends way too much to ignore them for work."

"What if you work with us?"

"Then is it really so bad to be a workaholic?"

"Yes. Because we'll quit working and go do stuff, and even when you hang out with us you'll be thinking about work, and if you have a husband or boyfriend, they won't enjoy it either," I said. Holly was staring at me.

"We're talking hypothetically, Maddi. I'm not actually a workaholic," Holly reminded me. Mickie laughed. Probably at one of our faces, because she most likely didn't understand what we were talking about.

"I know. I was talking hypothetically too." I wasn't lying when I said that, but apparently no one believed me.

"Sure, Maddi," Luke said. I gave up, knowing that with six people (Mickie didn't count in this situation) disbelieving me, I couldn't convince them. And it wasn't worth it, either. "This is good pizza, Mom."

"Thanks."

"What's for dinner tomorrow?" I questioned.

"I'm not sure. Possibly pancakes," Aunt Annie answered.

"Sounds good," Holly said.

"Yum," Mickie commented.

"So… how's Ben?" Aunt Annie asked. I rolled my eyes at Holly (I'd been doing a lot of that lately) before I answered. But I did answer. With a short comment, knowing there would be more questions.

June 26th

Dining Room

Interesting day, today was. It's fun to tease Ben. But I hate it when he teases me like that. I'm a hypocrite. Big deal. Shoot me. Whatever.

I'm happy. We had homemade pizza for dinner earlier. And I love Mom's homemade pizza. Luke helped make them. I think Mickie did, too. But I didn't 'cause I was still at work while they were doing this. That way we could eat earlier.

Maybe when I read this later in life, it'll be weird to read me excusing myself from my journal. But I like it. It means I might be able to remember the feelings I was feeling then. So… I gotta go so we can play dominoes! Luke begged to play, so now we're all playing, instead of just Aunt Annie, Uncle Chuck, Mom, and Dad playing after the rest of us have gone to bed.

"Why are they all of a sudden so friendly?" I asked Holly. My customers had good manners and were polite for once.

"I think they're all tourists who just got here for the weekend or something. That and I put the rude people in Sara's section."

"If they behave tomorrow like they are today, thanks for making me work tomorrow, Holly. You're great," I said. Holly smiled widely. I have to remember to say things like that more often. People feel special when they're complimented like that. I left to go back to my customers.

"Miss," a graying woman asked. She was there with two other women, both younger than her. The youngest was maybe a little older than me. I wondered if this was a grandmother-daughter-granddaughter trip.

"Yes?"

"We'd like to order now," she said.

"Okay, one second," I replied, pulling out my notebook and pen, then nodding for them to order.

"I'd like a Trapper Burger, medium well, please," the grandmother stated.

"Grilled Rosemary Chicken, please," the daughter said.

"Veal Meatloaf, please," was the granddaughter's order.

"Okay. I'll go put in these orders," I replied, collecting their menus. I saw a big group coming in the gate, and Holly was bringing them to my section. "Laura?" I called when I saw her inside.

"What, Maddi?"

"A big group just came in a minute ago, and I have to go take their drink order. Could you run this to the kitchen?"

"Sure. Good luck," she said, smiling.

"Actually, most of my customers have been good today. Good luck to you, too, I told her. Then I made my way outside again. "Hi, I'm Maddi, and I'll be your server today. What would you like to drink? We have Coke products," I greeted the ten people in my big group. They ordered a variety of drinks.

"Okay. I'll go get those for you," I told them, walking away. I brought the drinks in two trips, scared that I would spill them all if I carried ten drinks at once. After all, some of my clumsiness still remained. I think it started in seventh grade, when I broke or dislocated multiple body parts, fell up stairs, and tripped on flat surfaces. Falling when I saw Ben for the first time was proof that I was still clumsy, like it or not.

"Hey, Ben."

"Hi, Maddi."

"Are you staying today?" I asked.

"No. I'm sorry, I can't. Are you working tomorrow?"

"Yeah. I wasn't planning on it, but Holly volunteered us."

"What about Sunday?"

"We're probably packing, because we leave Monday. I was going to go to church Sunday this week. And my family would probably love me going then. But I could go tomorrow…" I suggested.

"Don't," he replied.

"Do it," Holly said, suddenly in the conversation. "I don't want to be all alone Sunday morning."

"Okay, fine," I agreed. "We should all do something Sunday morning."

"Like what?" Holly asked.

"We never actually rode horses that long," I started, turning to Ben and smiling.

"We could do that. Is that okay, Holly?"

"Yeah," she replied. I wondered if it actually was, because her smile seemed a little fake now. But I let it go.

"Be at Dufina at around half-past ten Sunday morning," I said to Ben.

"Remind me tomorrow," he told me.

"Sure," I agreed.

"Bye, Maddi."

"Bye." I turned my face up for a kiss, and he didn't disappoint me. Mr. Poe, on the other hand... "Bye," I whispered again, half shoving him out of the restaurant.

"Maddi! I told you at the beginning of the summer the rules!"

"I know. There's thirty-eight rules," I replied.

"And you just broke number thirty-eight!" he exclaimed. "I could fire you for not following the rules you agreed to follow!"

"I know. I'm sorry. But I was wondering if I could go now? My customers want my attention," I said, gesturing to a couple who was waving for me to come over.

"Fine. I guess you're only working one more day anyway, and it'd be pointless to fire you."

"Thanks. Bye, Mr. Poe!" I called as I headed over to my customers. That was dangerous. He's really fond of his rules!

Devon Warriner   ----------   Get Over it

June 27th
Pink Bedroom

Is it just me, or is Mr. Poe excessively creepy sometimes? He'll get all bent out of shape and wacko about his rules one minute, and then another decide to show that he has a heart and not fire you for being slow because you're in shock and upset. I wonder if maybe one of his role models is Donald Trump? He's the guy that always says "You're fired!", I think. With the finger-pointing on that show... not that I watch it... *The Apprentice*. Is that show even still on? I don't know. I only know that Mr. Poe is creepy and that Mickie wants my attention. Gotta go!

"Morning, Mickie," I greeted.

"Hey, Maddi."

"Whatcha doing?"

"Playing with the logs," she replied. She was on the floor in the family room playing with the Lincoln Logs that Luke and I had found at least five years ago in the closet below the stairs. I could tell they were really old, because there were pieces I didn't have when Luke and I had a set of Lincoln Logs. A lot of stuff was hidden in that closet, but we only liked those Lincoln Logs.

"Are you having fun?" I asked.

"Yeah."

"Are you making a house?"

"Yes."

"It doesn't have windows," I said.

"I can't make them."

"Do you want help?"

"Yes, please." So I taught her how to make windows with the Lincoln Logs. Holly came in a bit later and played with us. She volunteered to be the few people on horses we had, and I said I'd be the Indians that were in there. There were green army men soldiers in the box too. Then again, the Indians and their teepees probably didn't belong there either. Or the other people, or the horses, or the carts they pulled. But whatever.

"Do you want to be the soldiers, Mickie?" Holly offered.

"No."

"Do you want to be the people on horses or the Indians?" I asked.

"No. I want to knock over the buildings," she stated.

"Okay. Just randomly or when we put people in them?"

"When Indians run into them," she said.

"Okay." We played like that for a bit more until I glanced at my watch and realized that Holly and I had to go. "Mickie, I'm sorry, but we have to go," I told her. "Come on Holly," I said, pulling her up from the floor.

"Bye," Holly called.

"Bye, Holly. Bye, Maddi!" Mickie replied.

"So how are your customers?" Holly asked me when I went to take a break from them.

"Eh. Most of them are like yesterday, some of them are bad. It's okay, I don't mind."

"Well, here comes a *really* bad one. Want him in your section?" Holly asked when she saw Ben walking up the sidewalk.

"Duh," I said.

"Now, that's rude, Maddi," Ben remarked.

"You sound like my mother. Come on," I told him, glancing at Holly to make sure it was okay. I didn't bother grabbing a menu for him. He didn't need one, with all the days he'd been here.

"Your day been good?" he asked.

"Yup. Except for a few bad customers."

"Well, I hope I don't make it worse."

"Like you could," I replied.

"Well…"

"Don't you dare," I told him. I glanced around. Of course someone wanted me. "Gotta go."

"Excuse me, miss?" a woman in a pink Mackinac Island sweatshirt was trying to get my attention.

"Yes?"

"Are there restrooms here?" she asked. I wanted to laugh really hard. Of course there are restrooms in a restaurant. No, we serve beverages, but if someone has to use the restroom because of these, we make them hold it or go someplace else. But I kept from laughing.

"Yes. Go in those doors," I said, pointing to the doors that led inside. "Go all the way to the back of the restaurant and you'll see them."

"Thank you," the woman replied. I walked away laughing.

"You're happy. What's funny?" Holly asked.

"Someone just asked if there were restrooms here," I told her. She laughed harder than I had, which made me laugh harder. Sometimes laughing is a vicious circle. But we got ourselves under control once Holly saw Mr. Poe staring at us.

"Some people are really silly," she said.

"You can say that again," I agreed. "Talk to you later, Holly. Too many people want my attention today. They should all get dogs. Then they'll get plenty of attention," I joked.

"Be nice and stay positive, Maddi," Holly suggested.

"Thanks!" I called back.

June 28th

Outside Ste. Anne's (before Mass)

    Holly and I turned in our uniforms today! It felt so great to get rid of it. I don't have to wear orange anymore! I don't mind having an orange bike. It's more like a rusty orange, and it's pretty. But I hated wearing that bright orange! And now I don't have to! Yes!

    I told Ben about the lady who asked if there were restrooms. I described her face, which was really funny. She looked kind of insulted when she asked, probably thinking about how if we didn't, she'd have to leave her dinner and find somewhere else to go, or maybe thinking about having to hold it. She was hilarious. I love customers like that. Who act really dumb by accident and just make me laugh. It makes the day less stressful. And it's funny. Ooh! Gotta go, church starts in five minutes!

"Morning everybody," I said when I passed most of them in the dining room. Everyone but Mom and Aunt Annie were sitting at the long table. Most of the chairs they were sitting in were broken because they were old and weaker than they should be.

"Good morning, Maddi. We thought we'd have breakfast together before church," Aunt Annie said from the kitchen.

"Oh. What are we having?" I asked.

"Pancakes, eggs, and sausage," Uncle Chuck answered.

"Ew," I automatically said.

"You don't like pancakes and eggs?" Holly questioned.

"No, I was talking about the sausage. I hate breakfast meat."

"Oh," she replied.

"You're crazy," Mickie stated. Aunt Annie started to tell Mickie to be nice.

"It's okay, Aunt Annie. I am crazy," I told her. But she kept telling Mickie to mind her manners. Breakfast was ready soon after that. We were sitting at the table for a long time after we were done talking, until most everyone excused themselves to go get ready for church. Ben arrived just before they were going to leave. Aunt Annie looked at me and raised her eyebrows.

"Oh, please. We're not doing anything but horseback riding!" I exclaimed as Mom turned around and looked at me that way too.

"Holly's going too?" Mom asked.

"Yes, of course," I replied.

"Okay, have fun," she told us. Then they all left on their bikes, with the exception of Mickie who rode in the trailer that was attached to Uncle Chuck's bike.

"Holls! It's okay. Horses aren't scary!" I called. But then I mumbled, "for the most part," under my breath. Holly was going to get on a horse first, so we could encourage her. We hadn't told Andy what horses we wanted yet.

"You two get on one first!" she told me.

"Okay. Andy? Can we have Twilight and Ash?"

"Sure. I'll go get them," Andy replied. Holly was trying to mount a mare named Meg who was supposed to be good for beginners who might be nervous. Meg was chestnut brown. Her tail and mane were just a bit darker, and her eyes were a deep, dark brown. Meg wasn't the problem. Holly was just too scared to get on. Andy came back with the horses and helped me mount. I didn't really need it, because my legs were long and could get to the stirrup just fine, but it was helpful. Ben mounted quickly, while Holly was still standing on the ground holding Meg's reins, too scared to get on. After two more failed attempts at mounting, I called out to her.

"We could do something else, you know!" I suggested. Holly's face set in determination.

"No. I want to do this," she said firmly. She tried to mount one more time, and this time made it. I was reminded, for some odd reason, of one of the cheers the cheerleaders at Luke's Rocket Football games cheered. *"Hustle, hustle, hustle! Move it, move it, move it! All you have to do is put your mind to it."*

"Ready, Holly?" I asked.

"No," she called back. Andy was telling her how to make Meg walk and go a little faster, then how to stop. She tried it a little bit, and answered me again. "As ready as I'll ever be."

"Don't worry, Holly. It'll get easier as you actually do it," Ben told her. We set out on the road so we could get to the trails. We were in a line with Ben at the front and me in the rear. I was behind Holly to make sure nothing happened. If something really bad did, I probably wouldn't be much help, but if she got stuck, I could help with that.

"You're doing great, Holly!" I told her.

"Maddi, do you want to take the same trail as last time, or a different one?" Ben called back to me.

"I don't know. Maybe a different one," I replied.

"Different one it is," he said. The land we rode through was really pretty. Trees were on either side of us, but they weren't a thick forest, so we could still see through them. There were some fallen, dead trees leaning on the ground or on branches of younger trees, but most of the trees were alive and beautiful. I'm not some tree identification expert, so I couldn't say what kind of trees they were, but they were tall and green. Like most trees. The trail was just dirt, and the sides were still littered with brown, crackly, long fallen leaves. Every once in a while a horse would step on them, but we were mostly quiet. It was fun, and more peaceful than last time Ben and I rode horses. All of a sudden, a flock of birds flew off, spooking Holly's horse. Ben quickly got the horse to calm down so we could continue.

"I heard this story last summer about a spooked horse. A man was riding his bike with a big blue tube on his back. A horse pulling a carriage spooked and broke part of the carriage," Ben told us. I started laughing. "What?" he asked.

"Well, that was my dad," I told him when I stopped laughing.

"Really?" he said disbelievingly.

"Yes. That was my dad. We were all scared it would be a story in the newspaper."

"It wasn't."

"I know. They did have a story about a plastic bag spooking a horse downtown, though," I replied.

"Are we almost back yet?" Holly asked, interrupting.

"Why? Have you filled your quota of horse riding for today?" I asked.

"Actually, yes. I'm ready to be done now," she replied.

"Well, then, yes, we're almost back to the stables," Ben answered. "We can be back in a few minutes."

"Thanks," Holly said.

June 29th

Living Room

I'm sad that we're leaving tomorrow. I don't want to go home. This summer has been amazing!

We packed most of our clothes, and started the laundry for towels and stuff like that that we used. We're washing sheets tomorrow morning before we leave, so anything that has to be washed otherwise has to be washed tonight. We also just tore up the puzzle. Yes, we completed it this summer (it's been getting harder and harder to complete each year), which makes me happy. But it makes me feel more sad when we break it up to put back in its box. It means we're leaving.

I'm going to miss this place until we're back next year. I'll especially miss Ben. I'll even miss my job, and Nick and Anna, even though I only met them once. This is a really bittersweet time. I mean, I'm going home, to the people I missed there. But now I'm leaving here, and I'm going to miss the people I met here. Now excuse me, I have to go cry. Goodnight (to myself).

I woke up really early, realizing that I had to break up with Ben. I can't do long-distance relationships. I've seen people try them. They never work, and the stress is always huge.

I started crying as I opened my phone and pressed the number two for a couple seconds. Once my phone showed *"Calling Ben"* with his picture, I sobbed. Telling myself to calm down, counted to ten, breathing slowly. He answered when I was about to say seven.

"Ben, I need to meet you," I sobbed. "Downtown. This morning."

"When and where?" he asked, concerned.

"We're taking the one o'clock ferry. Meet me at twelve-thirty at Arnold dock?"

"Yeah, sure." I felt terrible now.

"I have to go." I waited a beat. "Bye."

"Bye, Maddi. I love you," he said. I chocked back a sob and hung up. This was going to be painful. Holly didn't need to know I was breaking up with Ben, so I walked to the small bathroom, washed my face the best I could with those faucets (they were maybe a centimeter away from the rim of the sink, and were separate "hot" and "cold" levers that were usually just cold), and went downstairs to help finish packing. We had already packed the clothes, food that was coming back with us, and most of Mickie's toys. Mostly all that was left was washing sheets and putting things on the luggage cart for the dray. I grabbed a gray bin with food in it and put in on the cart. Seeing as Luke told me to go away and they had everything under control, I walked back upstairs and stripped mine and Holly's beds. I gave the sheets to Mom as she passed with the other sheets. There was nothing more to do!

"Ben, I can't do this," I told him.

"Do what?" he asked.

"Long-distance relationships. You could be going across the country, and I can't travel to see you. And it isn't fair to you. You'll be in college. You'll want college girls," I sobbed.

"College girls? The ones that get drunk and go to parties all the time? The ones who are on scholarships and need to study all the time? The girls in between those kinds? Nah. Not interested. You're who I want," he said. His little speech made me sob more.

"Ben… Those are stereotypes," I said, crying. I knew that even though I was the one doing the breaking-up, I would still be the one throwing things across the room later.

"I know. Sorry. If you want to break up, we can, but I was hoping not too. We just got back together." I stared at the sadness in his eyes. It was a sadness I had seen before, and I knew it was reflected in my eyes, too. I couldn't take it anymore. I wiped my tears away and started walking the other way. "I'm taking that as a break-up sign," I heard him say. I wanted to turn around and hug him, at least, but I didn't let myself, thinking it was for the better.

Since Holly gets carsick, and Luke was complaining about last time, I was stuck in the backseat. Which was fine with me. I sat staring out the window until we had dropped Holly off and got home. After we somewhat unloaded, I went up to my room and collapsed on my bed, crying. My phone rang after maybe ten minutes.

"Hello?" I said, trying to sound normal.

"Hi. Maddi, do you want to come hang out?" Emily asked.

"No. I don't really feel the best."

"Oh. Okay. Hope you feel better soon!"

"Bye, Emily."

"Bye! See you sometime soon, right?"

"Yeah." Then we both hung up, and I drifted off to sleep.

My phone ringing woke me up the next day. Looking at the screen, I knew it was Holly calling me.

"Hey, Maddi. Guess what?" Holly said as soon as I answered my phone.

"I don't know," I replied glumly.

"I'm in the emergency room."

"Why?" I asked, starting to cry again. I was seeing flashbacks to when Bridget was in the hospital.

"I think I broke my ankle."

"Really?" I asked, thinking about and seeing something completely different than Holly and my room.

"Yeah, it really hurts. I fell playing basketball. Well, I did more than…" Holly answered.

"Oh! Sorry, Holly, I *have* to go!" I shouted, as the sobs came harder. I realized exactly why she looked familiar.

July 1st
My Bedroom

I know why that lady looked familiar! The African American woman with the green tank top and white Capri's! She's a nurse at the hospital. One of the nurses who cared for Bridget for the hour she was in the hospital. I saw her at least five times while I was in the room with Bridget. Ohh!!

The phone rang. My phone. I answered it, still crying. I was surprised my eyes hadn't come out yet. Three days of crying. Yeah, three days.

"Maddi? Are you okay?" Holly asked, concerned. I thought about that.

"I'm fine," I mumbled into the phone.

"You don't sound it. You haven't talked to Emily since we first got back on Monday, and you haven't talked to me since Tuesday. It's Thursday, Maddi. That's a long time," she replied. "No, I'm coming over." I hung up the phone after she did. But a minute later the music to *Crazy Frog* started playing.

"Hey, Em, can I call you back? Holly's coming over, and I need to make her leave."

"I know," Emily said simply.

"You know what?"

"I know Holly's coming over, I am too. Bye," Emily said as I heard the "ding-dong" of the doorbell.

"Come in, Emily, Holly," Mom welcomed my friends. "Maddi's upstairs."

"Maddi!" Holly called as my best friends came up the stairs. Their faces peered in the doorway.

"What are you doing, sitting in bed?" Emily questioned.

"I don't deserve to live!" I wailed, tears springing forward in my eyes. Holly and Emily exchanged a look.

"And why not?" Holly asked.

"I had *fun!* My best friend died this year, and I had *fun!* I didn't even wear black to mourn for the loss of her! I'm a terrible best friend!" I choked out between sobs.

"Okay, that's seriously it!" Holly yelled. She grabbed my cell phone and opened it. I couldn't tell what she was doing. Well, I could, it was ringing on speakerphone.

"Maddi?" Ben answered his phone after only a few rings. Holly put it off speakerphone, and Emily grabbed it.

"No. I'm Maddi's friend, Emily. You must be Ben."

"Hey, I'm here, too!" Holly shouted.

"Well, I have something to tell you. Maddi's depressed," Emily informed him. It was hard to hear only half a conversation.

"Break up..." I heard through my phone.

"No, she's depressed because of Bridget," Emily paused to let that sink in. "Bridget died in February. Maddi seems to be under the impression that she can't have any fun, so she feels guilty." Emily handed the phone to me.

"Maddi?" Ben asked.

"Yes?" I croaked. My sobs had stopped.

"No speaking, just listen, okay?" Not waiting for my answer, he moved on. "So Bridget died. It's not your fault, and *not* that huge deal you think it is! She was your best friend. She still can be. It's not your fault she died, and she wouldn't want you to punish yourself. How do I know? Friends are like that. Bridget would want you to enjoy life with or without her. Now, you're Catholic. Offer it to God. Just tell Him you don't know why Bridget died, but ask Him to help you trust Him and deal with it the right way. It's as simple as that, just pray about it!" Ben exclaimed. I had listened to his whole speech.

"How do you know?" I asked.

"Well, I didn't tell you this before, but my dad died about five years ago. It was really hard on my mom and me, but we got through it," he told me. He sounded slightly sad and I wished I could be talking to him in person, so I could at least give him a hug. "Our life changed afterwards. Mom stopped riding horses, because that was something they had done together since they had dated. But with time, everything got back to normal. Well, the *new* normal of not having dad around. Sometimes I really miss him, but most of the time now I just remember all of the great times we had together. We're doing fine now and I do pray a lot to help me."

Ben's voice was soft and warm and was so comforting to me. "So what do you say when you pray," I asked. I decided to just trust this guy that I loved.

"You can talk to God however you want to, do what is comfortable for you, but just roughly, you could start with something like, 'God, I don't know why Bridget died, but help me to trust you and deal with it in the right way," Ben said. I repeated what he said, adding a sign of the cross and an amen, and I actually felt a lot lighter. Something had lifted. The weight of the death lightened. I wasn't the only one to carry it, I realized. "Oh, by the way, I'm going to Western Michigan University," Ben informed me.

"That's great!" I exclaimed. "That's like, forty minutes away!" He laughed.

"Does that mean we're back together?"

"Yes!" I exclaimed in response.

"Okay, so… I have to go," Ben said.

"Okay, bye! Love you!"

"Love you, too, Maddi." He hung up.

"So…" Emily drew out the word like a question. "What happened?"

"Oh. I feel better," I told them. I actually smiled for the first time in a few days.

"That's great!" Holly exclaimed, hugging me. Emily joined in too.

"I love you guys. You always look out for me," I stated.

"Hey, what are friends for?" Emily questioned. I laughed.

"True friends," Holly added. I smiled again, then hugged them tighter. Somehow I knew with God and my friends, I could make it through anything!

Maddi Andrews
English 12
Hour 3
9/5/08

What I Did Over the Summer

    The "What I Did Over The Summer" report is cliché. Usually I dread this kind of report, but this year is different. I did not go on some world travel vacation, just my normal trip to Mackinac Island. But this past summer has been so different from my other summers – and so much better.

    Bridget was my best friend. She was the greatest artist I knew, and a good storywriter, too. She was always a little distracted, a little slow to catch on, but she was so good with any details. Ask her to describe someone, and you would have gotten the fullest description ever. She was so cool that way.

    Every summer, Bridget and her family would spend a week with my family on Mackinac Island. We would bike around, eat out for lunch, make dinner at the cottage, shop, and eat fudge. It is always so much fun to go on vacation with a close person that is not related to you. However, she will not be able to come this year. No, it is not her parents' fault, or her own. Unfortunately this year is just how it is. This summer was going to be the best one ever. A couple years ago, we convinced our parents to let us ride horses. We were going to do so much more this time. We were going to cook dinner one night (because it was going to be fun), ride horses by ourselves (well, we would have a guide, but no parents), bike around the island by ourselves, and have our own adventure. All that changed a few months ago. I used to look forward to this trip, but now I am dreading it. Part of my heart died with Bridget that night, February 22, when a drunk driver smashed into her car and fatally injured her. I almost went to Mackinac alone this year. After all, how could it be the same without Bridget? But I needed someone to help me see the sights, do the things Bridget and I were going to do, and help me deal with her being gone. So I am bringing Holly, another great friend, but it will not be the same. We will not have the same freedom, because she has only been to Mackinac Island once, during our fourth grade trip there, and does not know the lay of the land. I am going to miss Bridget. My life will never be the same. Every day will be different.

Bridget's funeral was a few days after the accident. I could not stand to be in the room. I have been to several funerals, so I thought I could handle this one, but it was different. Most of the funerals I have been to, I did not really know the person, or I was too young to understand. The only other person I was close to whose funeral I went to was my Grandma Katie's. I was only three then, so I did not understand what we were doing. As soon as I walked up to Bridget's casket, I started crying. Her big cappuccino-colored eyes were closed, and her brown hair was neatly arranged. She was ghostly pale. I had to leave because I was going to cry. Actually, I was going to sob and I felt like screaming. So I said my final words to her. Then I leaned over the edge to kiss her head like a parent might do to a child to say goodnight, but I was saying goodbye. Not even for just a short while, but goodbye for forever. I ran into the bathroom and cried the rest of the funeral. My friends Holly and Emily soon appeared to comfort me. Neither of them were as close to Bridget as I was, but they felt my pain too. No words were needed between the three of us. We just sat on the floor, in each other's company, feeling a comfort no words can give. Bridget meant a lot to me, nobody can understand how much. No one will ever understand how deep our friendship was, how deeply we were connected. On February 22, Bridget died, and so did part of me. I hope and pray that this does not happen to anyone else. No one should have to go through this suffering when they are only seventeen years old.

This is what I felt and wrote in May earlier this year. But in June, there was another life changing event. This time, it was helpful.

I went on my usual Mackinac vacation. But we stayed on the island for almost a month. Holly and I were hired by the Gate House restaurant. While we were looking for jobs, I met a guy. He made me laugh, and was wonderful. He was my boyfriend until we broke up when I left, and a little bit in the middle of the month. When I got home, I stayed in my bed sobbing for a long time. Even though I had nothing to do with it, I blamed myself for Bridget's death, and would not let myself have fun. But when I got home, I realized I had fun with Ben (my boyfriend). So I apologized to Bridget over and over, crying. My friends, Holly and Emily, came over to my house when I would not answer their calls. They stole my phone and called Ben, so he could help too. Since I had not told Ben any of this, they explained the situation, and gave me my phone. They forced me to talk to my ex-boyfriend. Together, all three of them taught me that I cannot blame myself for things I have no control over, and that I can mourn, but I have to move on. Bridget would want that for me. So now I am enjoying life again without all the guilt, and I hope that I am back on the track I was on before Bridget died. I hope that now, if she is watching me, she would smile. Wonderful friends can change lives. Mine certainly changed my life.

Devon Warriner   ----------   Get Over it

The Author

Devon is a high school student who enjoys her time as a "fudgie," or tourist, on Mackinac Island in the summer. She can be found reading at almost any time, and has had a love for writing since she was a little kid. She lives in Michigan with her Family.

Printed and Published by
2 Moon Press Book Publishing
800publishing.com